A DOG NAMED DUKE

*True Stories of German Shepherds at Work
with the Law*

A DOG
NAMED DUKE

True Stories of German Shepherds
at Work with the Law

Leo A. Handel

J. B. Lippincott Company

PHILADELPHIA   **NEW YORK**

To My Father

Contents

Introduction

Early in 1963 a news photographer took a picture in a Southern town of the United States that was soon to appear on the covers of magazines, and on the front pages of newspapers all over the world. It was the picture of an ugly, ferocious animal baring powerful, sharp teeth and straining on its leash in a furious attack. The animal was a German shepherd. Its target was a scared man, a Negro taking part in an anti-segregation demonstration.

The captions to this picture varied with the points of view of the editors. "Police Dog Used in Race Riot," stated the more conservative papers. "Police Brutality," screamed other headlines. For many people this picture of a fierce police dog was their first knowledge of an organized Canine Corps in action, and large segments of the population became aware that dogs are used as a regular force by police departments in the United States.

But this first impression of a police dog could hardly have been more distorted. True, some Canine Corps dogs are trained and successfully used in riot control. However, this constitutes only one of many functions and, in the overall picture, a very minor one.

Actually the police dog-handler team represents one of the most successful and appealing combinations in the man-dog relationship, a relationship that can be traced back thousands of years.

Sometime, somewhere in the ancient world a man and a dog encountered each other and stopped for a moment to look into each other's eyes. A hairy hand may have found its way to the soft fur between the dog's ears in a clumsy but genuine gesture of affection and need. A gesture that may have been returned with a timid lick of a rough tongue and a tentative beat of a tail. The man and the dog decided to form a friendship, an act that was duly engraved on the wall of a cave for all posterity to see—a friendship destined to last until the end of time.

The modern Canine Corps of some of our police departments is a crowning achievement of this development. The combination of a strong, intelligent, and well-trained animal and an expert criminologist became a valuable team for crime detection and crime prevention in a great number of major police departments all over the world. And many smaller constabularies in less populated communities and rural areas would not want to do without their dogs.

The system has proved itself a total success. Police dogs, completely fearless in the defense of their masters, have given their lives for this cause. And one instance is known of a police officer who was killed while trying to save his dog.

The dog-man combination in police work includes an impressive array of talents, powers, and capabilities. The police dog's greatest asset is his acute sense of smell. It is estimated that this is about forty times as strong as a man's. Also, the dog's hearing is much keener than that of a human. The animal's agility makes it possible to enter places a person could not reach or would be slow in reaching. A dog is a faster runner than his handler. Aided by his senses of smell and hearing, the animal can move around in darkness without difficulty and locate persons or objects.

The police dog is a very strong animal. The jaws of a well-developed German shepherd can exert five hundred to six hundred pounds of pressure per square inch. Those jaws can easily break a man's arm and the criminal is well aware of this power. Consequently, the mere presence of a dog can lead to an uncomplicated arrest.

The police dog has unflinching loyalty. In the large majority of cases a dog is assigned to a single handler. He lives with his master and his master's family. In case of danger the dog's loyalty is undivided, uncompromising, complete.

A police dog working with his handler acts on command as a gun responds to the pressure of the trigger. Of course, a dog should not be used for attack unless this is the last resort, but if the necessity arises a dog, like a gun, can be an awe-inspiring weapon. Sometimes a dog causes greater fear than a gun in an officer's hand. Also, an attacking dog can be stopped in his tracks by a call from his handler, while a bullet is stopped only by its target.

The psychological impact of police dogs on criminals is tremendous. Apprehended by an officer, a person who realizes that one careless movement may bring on an attack by the officer's canine partner is a meek subject indeed. Exceptions to this rule are rare. Also, the dog may be responsible for a real conflict. Some criminals who hate police officers are very partial to dogs. Suddenly, when confronted both by a man in uniform and a dog, they will be confused and torn in their feelings.

At least one police dog has made substantial contributions to alcoholic reform. He was trained to lick the faces of drunks to awake them. When the drunk opened his eyes and found a dog's big teeth shining at him, he had a strong incentive to stop drinking.

The law-abiding citizens of a community accept police dogs whole-heartedly, especially in high-frequency crime areas. So police dogs frequently become excellent public relations instruments.

Today, practically all police dogs are male German shepherds. The breed, somewhat resembling its ancestral wolf (hence "wolf dog") in conformation and appearance, is characterized by power, agility, balance, and coordination. Ideally the dog stands twenty-five inches high at the shoulders; weighs between seventy-five and eighty-five pounds; has a cleancut head with powerful jaws and erect, moderately pointed ears; a smooth, slightly wavy outer coat; a protective inner coat; and a long, bushy tail. The color varies in shades and mixtures of black and brown.

The German shepherd is distinguished for his working qualities, his responsiveness to training, keen sense of smell, high order of intelligence and ability to exercise judgment. He has been used effectively in military work and as a "seeing eye" companion for the blind. The breed originated in Germany and was introduced in the United States in 1904. Interestingly enough, the German name for this dog has been for years "Polizeihund," meaning police dog. The British use the name "Alsatian" or "Alsation wolf dog."

It was not until 1946, when six dogs were taken into the service of the London Metropolitan Police, that the first serious attempt was made to use a dog as extra aid to the policeman. But these dogs were employed in the suburban areas as patrol dogs and were little more than companions to their handlers.

When police dogs were first brought to Central London in 1948, they achieved spectacular successes in Hyde Park where the prevalent crime of handbag stealing was practically eliminated. Good work of this kind, plus a number of arrests as the result of tracking, searching for, and pursuing criminals, encouraged the use of dogs on general purpose work throughout the whole of the London Metropolitan Police District.

The number of successful results achieved by the London Dog Section has risen progressively each year. Perhaps the most pleasing feature of these achievements is that more and more incidents are being brought to a successful conclusion through the work of the dog itself. This is particularly true in the field of tracking.

The London Metropolitan Police District, which extends over an area of some 740 square miles, varies in character from the open country on the outskirts to the crowded, closely built-up streets of Central London. It includes large housing estates, commercial areas, warehouses, docks, public gardens, and parks. The use of police dogs has been progressively developed to deal with the many different law enforcement problems which are bound to arise from such varied types of terrain.

At this time, the number of dogs employed by the London Police amount to almost 200 animals. A recent report, when the active strength of the "dog force" was 160, showed that in the three months' report period the dog units were credited with the following accomplishments: 71 arrests made by dogs, 344 arrests made with dogs' assistance, 9 missing persons found, and 17 items of missing properties found.

The London dogs are not kept in the background to wait for emergencies to arise. In order to obtain their full value as both a deterrent and detection force, they are kept out on regular patrol beats.

In their endeavors to form new Canine Corps, numerous police departments in the United States and other countries have requested and received technical advice from the London Metropolitan Police. In some instances law enforcement personnel visited England for orientation in this line of police work. In other cases the London

Police sent dogs and trainers abroad. After thorough indoctrination, the trainers return home and the dogs remain in their new surroundings.

The police department of Baltimore, Maryland, is the pioneer for the use of dogs in the United States. Two dog-handler teams were put into operation in December, 1956, on an experimental basis. The Baltimore Canine Corps was credited with over five hundred arrests in its first year of full operation. The presence of dog patrols around Johns Hopkins and other Baltimore hospitals, as an example, have reduced to a minimum the formerly serious problem of the accosting and robbing of nurses and hospital visitors. Now the Baltimore Canine Corps consists of thirty-five men and forty dogs.

The number of police dog units in the United States is growing steadily, and there are fundamental reasons for this development.

The problem of providing citizens with adequate police protection grows greater with each passing year. As the need for wider coverage by policemen increases, it becomes an economic problem to provide sufficient personnel. Although there is a constant expansion of police functions, the number of men available to the forces does not always increase. As a consequence, police protection is often spread very thin. One-man patrols on foot or in radio cars become necessary under conditions where two-men teams would be more desirable. The growing dangers to officers working alone indicates that some measures have to be taken to protect these men, without a substantial increase of community budgets. Alternative methods have to be developed.

An inexpensive but reliable partner can be made available to the policeman. That is, of course, the trained police dog. The powerful animal on alert in the squad car or ready for action next to the officer, trained to attack at the sight of a gun in the suspect's hand, can prevent many attacks on lone policemen, some of which result in death.

The dog does not replace a second officer, but he offers his unique talents to the officer who would otherwise be working alone. The criminal, in many cases, has all the odds in his favor—initiative, darkness, sometimes number. But the presence of a trained police dog may neutralize the criminal's advantages and turn the odds in the favor of the officer.

There can be no way of evaluating the feelings of comfort to a policeman working alone at night when he can order his dog into a black alley and know that a dangerous presence will be announced with a deep growl, a sound that turns dangerous persons into meek cowards. He can have his dog patiently but alertly watch a routine traffic arrest which might otherwise flare up in a viscious attack on the officer.

The trained police dog seems to develop an intuition about criminals—a sort of a sixth sense, which cannot be adequately explained. Dogs seem to have the ability to detect fear, perhaps smell the cold sweat of a person frightened by the presence of the police. On occasion, dogs point out criminals without any previous means of association.

To the officer his canine companion is not just "any" dog, nor, to the dog, is the officer just "any" man. The dog takes his commands from only *one* person. This prevents criminals from learning police dog commands and countermanding the initial order.

The dog has been used by man for centuries for such varying purposes as rescue work, as beasts of burden, for sport events, as war dogs and as aids for the blind. Bloodhounds and other dogs were used on occasion for certain tracking tasks.

It was only after World War II that the capabilities of the dog were used systematically as an integral element of major police departments. That period sparked the use of dogs in a number of roles. The armed forces of some countries used them as guard, attack, messenger and scout dogs. Some dogs were especially trained during the London blitz to locate people buried under the rubble of collapsed buildings. Later, such recovery work was also done by British Army dogs who were taught to find wounded soldiers on the battlefield.

As far as police work is concerned, it is known that as long ago as the fifteenth century the London constables patrolled with dogs. But the animals were probably used then more for companionship than for police work.

The Metropolitan London Police is probably the leading exponent in the training and employment of dogs. Between the two world wars Scotland Yard experimented with the use of bloodhounds, Labradors, boxers, Dobermans, Rottweilers, and German shepherds. It was first thought necessary to have different types of dogs and different types of training to produce dogs for specific tasks. But it has later been proved that a suitable dog can be trained as an "all-rounder," which is also more economical. The London Police came to the conclusion that the German shepherd has proved the most adaptable and the most reliable for police work.

The single-handler concept promotes also the unquestioning loyalty of the dog for his master. As a rule the dog lives with the handler and his family. The handler feeds him and devotes considerable time and effort, on and off duty, to caring for the animal. The dog's reliability when the chips are down is the result of this system.

The dog is expected to attack only when so ordered by his handler, when attacked himself, or when a suspect is trying to escape. The dog and the handler know that a ferocious growl and baring of teeth will control the criminal in most cases. The dog knows also that every person is to be treated gently until the situation forces him to the alternative.

A survey among police departments in the United States concerning their experience with police dogs showed, with few exceptions, an enthusiastic and favorable response. Most of the departments anticipated larger canine units due to their dogs' exemplary records. The criminal element of these cities was considerably hampered by the patrol dog units, and the general public soon accepted the animals as a welcome tool of the police force. Dogs have a favorable effect on police public relations. Negative publicity is produced only in areas were dogs are employed to control racial integration activities.

The use of police dogs in the United States is gradually emerging from the experimental stage and, in many instances, becoming part of police routine. The following major police departments in the United States operate effective canine units:

Alexandria, Virginia
Atlanta, Georgia
Baltimore, Maryland
Birmingham, Alabama
Boston, Massachusetts
Chicago, Illinois
Cleveland, Ohio
Dallas, Texas
Delaware State Police
Denver, Colorado
Houston, Texas
Jackson, Mississippi
Kansas City, Missouri
Kingman, Arizona
Las Vegas, Nevada
Miami, Florida

New Orleans, Louisiana
Philadelphia, Pennsylvania
Pomona, California
Reno, Nevada
Richmond, Virginia
St. Louis, Missouri
St. Paul, Minnesota
Salt Lake City, Utah
San Francisco, California
Springfield, Missouri
Washington, D.C.
Wichita, Kansas

Notable exceptions among the major police departments are New York City and Los Angeles. New York City used to have a canine unit but discontinued it.

Histories of famous police dogs are beginning to be recorded from all over the world—reports of incredible skill, courage, and loyalty. Famous dogs such as "Rex of Scotland Yard," "Dox" of the Italian Police, and "Xorro" of the Paris Sûreté have already achieved immortality in the history of crime.

It is quite possible that new training techniques will be responsible for even more remarkable feats, even though the principal value of the Canine Corps, as in the other areas of crime detection and prevention, is produced by everyday routine work.

But there is the intriguing thought that somewhere in the United States a bright-eyed German shepherd puppy is chasing his police dog father, a puppy that will grow into an intelligent, valuable police dog himself and join phenomenal members of the canine world, such as the British Rex III and the Italian Dox.

A DOG NAMED DUKE

*True Stories of German Shepherds at Work
with the Law*

1

Rex of Scotland Yard

On a misty April morning in 1950, a man walked into the Esher Kennels near London and took a long, scrutinizing look at a German shepherd. The dog, large for his twelve months, with black and tan markings and beautifully chiselled features, turned his clear, brown eyes in the direction of the man and looked at him steadily. The man knew, and he says so did the dog, that they were meant to accomplish great deeds together. And this, certainly, they did.

The man was Constable Arthur Holman of the London Metropolitan Police. The dog was "Rex III" or "Rex of Scotland Yard," as the British and many people outside the Isles soon would know him. The police officer and the animal fused themselves into the first great man-dog team in the annals of British criminology. Their activities accelerated the use of police dogs in England and in many other countries.

Early in 1950, Scotland Yard decided to step up the program for training dogs as an aid in crime detection and law enforcement. A directive was circulated, asking for police officers qualified to work with dogs. Holman volunteered immediately. He had had his own dogs since early youth and was said to have a way with animals. Holman's qualifications resulted in an immediate approval of his transfer and, without much delay, he was ordered to select "his" dog.

From that day in April, the German shepherd and his handler were hardly ever apart. For six years they were in constant service and credited with a total of 125 arrests for crimes ranging from petty thefts to armed robbery and murder. They were called upon at all hours of the day and night, in every condition of weather. In numerous cases Rex captured criminals after the police had failed. Rex III was the first dog to hunt for criminals with Scotland Yard's Flying Squad, and he was the first British dog to receive medals for bravery. His life was often in jeopardy. In his book, *My Dog Rex*, trainer Arthur Holman descibes in affectionate detail the years he worked with this amazing canine.

The education of Rex followed rather unorthodox methods by today's standards. Training manuals and rigid training schedules were not available at that time and Holman had to work mainly by ear. Even the basic police dog functions, as well as potential, were not yet defined. Arthur Holman's main ingredients of teaching consisted of patience, instinctive understanding and affection; qualities that were fully reciprocated by his animal.

Within a few months the dog's repertoire boasted an impressive array of actions essential for the successful execution of police work: "Sit" . . . "Crawl" . . . "Stop him" . . . "Track" . . . "Leave" . . . "Heel" . . . "Speak" . . . "Up" . . . "Stay" . . . "Find" . . . "Fetch." What impressed Holman just as much as the dog's ability to learn was the animal's continuous demonstration of plain common sense. With unfailing accuracy Rex could tell a member of the police from a suspect in situations where he had not been exposed to either before and where the police officer was a plain-clothes detective.

Holman succeeded in teaching the dog to respond to silent hand commands in addition to or instead of word commands. Rex was the first police dog who could take orders in this fashion, a capability that was to be useful on certain occasions.

Graduation exams for Rex and a number of other canine students were scheduled for July 14, 1950. Rex went through his prescribed tasks with effortless, almost contemptuous ease. He graduated as number one of the class of 1950 and was now an official member of the London Police Force.

Dope traffic constitutes only a minor law enforcement problem in Great Britain, as registered addicts may obtain narcotics upon prescription for about the same price as a bottle of aspirin. However, Scotland Yard wanted to find out whether or not dogs might be used to detect dope. Holman and Rex were selected for the experiment. After a few weeks of training the dog's nose became so sensitive that he could determine the presence of the minutest quantities of the narcotics placed well out of sight and reach. This was probably the first time in police history that this procedure was developed.

Rex's threatening fangs, his roaring growl, and massive build were invaluable assets in many police actions. To the suspects the German shepherd was undoubtedly an awesome picture. His handler knew that there was quite a bit of acting talent in the dog, who seemed to enjoy some of these performances. And Rex proved the value of this behavior. Only one suspect exposed to this formidable sight ever attempted to put up any resistance. This was a cornered Army deserter fortified with a stolen service revolver.

The man, it was determined, was hiding in a house on a certain street in London. A Criminal Investigation Division (C.I.D.) sergeant and a detective-constable were ordered to take the man into custody. They asked Holman and his dog to come along—"just in case."

The deserter was located and apprehended easily enough. It looked like a routine arrest, and the suspect left the house with the officers. Holman and Rex, as was their custom, had waited outside and there was no indication of any sort of difficulty.

Suddenly and unexpectedly the suspect became violent and broke away from the two officers. "Stop him!" Holman yelled to his dog as the deserter raced toward a side road. Holman, confident that the man would not get far, hurried in the same direction.

The man suddenly noticed that a police dog was closing in on him. To Holman's horror the deserter drew a revolver from the pocket of his overcoat, aimed at the dog, and fired. Luckily he missed Rex. The dog, with complete disregard of the danger, jumped up on the man, sinking his teeth in the gunman's right arm. At the same instant a second shot was fired but went wild due to the dog's action.

In the meantime the detective-constable caught up with the deserter and Holman ordered Rex to release the prisoner so that the policeman could complete the arrest. Rex obeyed. As the detective grabbed the gunman the latter made another unexpected and desperate try for escape. He jerked himself free and tried to run away.

"Stop him!" Holman ordered Rex again. But the dog

knew what he was expected to do even before he heard the command and bounded after the gunman.

The scene that followed will stay with Holman for his entire life. The deserter, looking back, saw the German shepherd coming at him. The man skidded to a stop, levelled the revolver at Rex, and waited calculatingly until the dog was about to leap. Then he pushed the gun into the dog's face, right between the eyes, and pulled the trigger. The shot reverberated through the narrow street. Rex turned a backwards somersault in midair and fell to the ground. There he lay motionless, without even uttering a whine.

Holman felt an icy claw of sadness reaching for his heart. His dog must be dead, shot right between the eyes.

The deserter had lost valuable seconds in turning, stopping, and shooting at the dog, and the detective-constable was able to catch up with the man and grab him. It was an irrevocable grip.

Holman, his legs lead-heavy, slowly approached his dog. But—before the man was at the dog's side, the animal suddenly trembled, lifted his head and staggered to his feet. As if drawn by an irresistible force, Rex turned in the direction of the scuffle which he could hear but could not see; his eyes were blinded by the white spots of the powder burns.

The handler ordered the animal to lie down and made sure that the gunman was rendered harmless. Then he knelt down next to his dog and examined him. Miraculously the bullet had missed and had merely grazed the dog's left ear. The dog had been knocked unconscious by the concussion, and the trouble with his eyes was only temporary.

But the German shepherd's most outstanding feat was probably the decisive part he played in the apprehension of what the London press came to call "The Phantom Car

Gang." Arthur Holman wrote a firsthand account of this event.

Toward the end of 1952, London was plagued by a gang of armed bandits. The targets were jewelry stores and radio and television shops. The criminals were clever operators who did not leave any evidence to aid the police in the investigation. In some instances the gang operated with a fast Jaguar, a Mark VII, and in one case the expertly driven car even got away from a pursuing police radio car.

Finally, Scotland Yard was able to determine that the Jaguar had been stolen from the Piccadilly area of London. The original license number ALT 820 had been changed to ALT 82. At last the police had something to go on.

It did not take long to locate the car in a garage belonging to a block of apartment houses in Notting Hill. The garage was rented from a woman who was not in any way involved with the criminals. It would have been an easy thing to apprehend the men on a car theft charge, but in order to obtain a conviction on the armed robberies, the suspects had to be caught with the stolen goods in their possession.

With the decision to stake out the garage, Constable Holman and his dog Rex came into the case, transferred for temporary duty with the Flying Squad. Holman was warned that the bandits were considered extremely dangerous; they had announced they would run down any policeman who tried to stop them.

While anticipating a rough time, Holman felt very proud that night when he and Rex made their way to the location of the stakeout. This was not only the first time the Flying Squad had asked for the support of a dog but also the head of this crack unit of the London police had specified Rex in his request.

Holman and some of the members of the Flying Squad made a careful reconnaissance of the block in Notting Hill from where the Phantom Car Gang started their raids. A bombed-out, roofless house offered a good vantage point for observation. Holman and Rex climbed to the top floor of the building to commence their lonely vigil.

The night was cold and damp. After an hour it started to drizzle. Holman thought of the many hours he had spent on duties similar to the current assignment. He looked gratefully at Rex, whose very presence made the task much easier, less dangerous, and less unpleasant.

As the night continued, the activity in this neighborhood decreased, with fewer cars, fewer pedestrians—and more boredom. Around midnight the sergeant in charge decided to call off the detail. A squad car took Holman and Rex to their home, where the man and animal thawed out in front of a fire.

But the next day at six in the evening, Rex and Holman were back on the job. It was colder; the drizzling rain had given way to frost. Yet this night patience and perseverance were destined to pay off. At around half past eight two men approached the garage where the Jaguar ALT 82 was located. After a few minutes' warm-up the car was driven out and soon disappeared.

Two detective-sergeants and a constable went into a huddle with Holman. The men prepared a plan to be put into effect upon the return of the car which, they assumed, would be used for another raid. The men were prepared to collect the criminals along with the stolen goods as evidence.

The Jaguar returned at half past ten. Holman and Rex started their predetermined action. They walked along the road past the apartments, giving the impression of a local resident taking his dog for a stroll.

The suspects parked the Jaguar, closed the garage door,

and turned to leave. The C.I.D. men left their observation posts, ran towards the two members of the Phantom Car Gang, and took hold of one of them. The other man tore away. Holman could see that the constable would not be able to catch up with him.

This was the task for Rex.

"Get him!" Holman commanded, and Rex catapulted away. The common sense of this dog dictated whom he was supposed to catch. After all, there were three policemen and two criminals on the scene. Still, Holman did not have to specify the dog's target.

The suspect, realizing a dog was pursuing him, increased his tempo. He had to get rid of the dog. Making a sharp turn, he climbed over a gate six feet high and disappeared from Holman's sight. Rex, without as much as losing a beat, jumped across the wall next to the gate. A short while later the chase was all over. Rex cornered the suspect who had run short of new territory.

Holman took the suspect back to the road where the sergeants were waiting with the other prisoner. The constable, who had attempted to follow Holman, had slipped and injured his right arm. One of the sergeants, too, had sustained an injury during the arrest of the first man, who had made a desperate attempt to get away.

The officers led the two suspects back to the garage where the Jaguar was parked, intending to search for stolen articles needed for the conviction. Suddenly two more men rushed from the garage. Seeing the police had their two accomplices under arrest, they attempted to make a getaway.

The Flying Squad men had to rely on Rex.

"Stop them!" ordered Holman.

The dog, probably expecting the command, practically flew after the two fugitives who had been swallowed up in the darkness. He stopped the first man in his tracks by jumping on his back and throwing him to the ground. He growled and threatened the man until he lay motionless and one of the sergeants came into sight to take over.

Then Rex raced after the second fugitive, overtook him in a few seconds, and grabbed the man's wrist with his teeth. The suspect's will to resist seemed to evaporate.

In a short while four prisoners were standing against a wall. In front of them, Rex saw to it that they stayed put. A sergeant left to call Scotland Yard for a car. Suddenly one of the suspects made another effort to get away. He broke loose, ran across the road, and climbed over a wall.

It was, again, a job for Rex. Upon Holman's command he took after the man. The dog scaled the wall and, after a few seconds, let out a fierce growl that told Holman that Rex had made contact with his target.

Soon the quartet of criminals was together again. They were picked up by a car from the Notting Hill Gate police station and safely transferred to jail.

A search of the Jaguar revealed a number of pieces of silverware valued at about five hundred English pounds, which had been stolen that night. With this evidence on hand the four members of the Phantom Car Gang were sent to prison with sentences ranging from eighteen months to four years.

Rex received a commendation from the judge and praise from the newspapers of London. He had indeed played a decisive role. Since two of the four police officers involved were injured at the beginning of the action, it can easily be seen that the gang may not have been caught at that time except for the courageous and intelligent action of Constable Holman and his dog.

Rex and his handler had always been the talk of the town. The dog's efficiency was demonstrated at meetings of police officers from England and other countries. Rex and Holman appeared numerous times on the BBC television network, doing their share to foster public relations of the London Police.

The most memorable demonstration of the dog's skill was a Command Performance for British Royalty, the highest possible tribute to the usefulness of police dogs. This event took place in April, 1951. The eight leading police dogs of the Force were presented to King George VI and Queen Elizabeth.

The demonstration went off smoothly. Rex and the seven other dogs showed routine police procedures which were required from the graduates of the canine basic training course. The performances culminated in two "solos" by Rex III—a "gun chase" and the finding of a man who was hiding in a tree near the area from where the royal party watched the action. Rex's matter-of-fact dealing with the situations drew a round of applause from the intrigued audience.

King George and Queen Elizabeth expressed the desire to meet Rex and his handler. Their Majesties walked over to Arthur Holman and Rex. Man and dog stood at rigid attention.

The Queen was the first to reach Police Constable Holman. "How does your wife like having a police dog at home?" she asked.

"My wife is very fond of the dog, Your Majesty," Holman managed to say. He was not accustomed to conversing with royalty. Rex, on the other hand couldn't have been more at ease. He showed his approval of the Queen with two quick beats of his tail.

"And how does the dog get on with your children?" continued the Queen.

"Extremely well, Your Majesty."

The Queen smiled warmly and turned to a member of her entourage. King George gave the dog a knowing look. There was no doubt that he had great admiration for the animal. "You have a very good-looking dog," he said. "I shouldn't like him after me."

The BBC evening news on October 8, 1956, opened with a tragic report: Rex had been put to sleep because of an incurable throat infection. He was only seven years old, very young for an Alsatian.

The passing of the dog left a void in his master's life, one never to be filled.

2

Dox of the Squadra Mobile

One day late in 1945, Signor Giovanni Maimone acquired a two-month-old German shepherd pup. This vivacious little bundle of unlimited energy bore the impressive name, "Dox von Coburger Land." Maimone, who was at that time serving with the police department of Turin, Italy, devoted every free hour to the care and training of his puppy. From the very beginning, the dog showed great intelligence, unusual agility and outstanding strength and stamina—the prerequisites for a police dog. Maimone felt that some of the unique talents of dogs could be used in law enforcement, and attempted to find a capable animal to prove his theory.

Dox's education proceeded much faster than anticipated. But in spite of all the initial encouragement, Giovanni Maimone had no idea that a budding world celebrity was bouncing at the end of the leash. Dox was destined to serve for fifteen years with police departments all over Italy. He ended his illustrious career as the top dog with Rome's famous crack police unit known as the "Squadra Mobile."

The dog and his master became regular participants in the most important Italian and European competitions. Dox received eight gold medals, and a great many silver medals, citations, and other awards for his winning performances at those matches. But he was not just a collector of medals. The thick, tawny fur of the long-haired German shepherd covered the ugly scars of nine bullet and knife wounds which the dog received in line of duty. Dox was responsible for 171 arrests, and there were times when the going was rough both for the dog and the police officer.

Dox was only eight months old when he and his master received their first assignment. One day in May, 1946, Officer Giovanni Maimone stood at attention in front of his superior.

"Capitano," said Maimone, "I ask for your permission to use my dog on the case . . ."

The captain looked up with surprise. "The jewelry store robbery?"

"Yes, sir," answered Maimone. "I believe Dox is ready."

"But isn't he much too young?" asked the captain consulting an index card.

"Sir, with your permission, I would like to put the dog to a test," countered the young police officer persuasively.

The captain hesitated for a moment. Then he made up his mind. "All right, you must know your dog. Give him a try. But be sure not to interfere with the investigation; this seems to be a complicated case."

"Thank you, sir. Don't worry. Dox is a very unusual

dog." This was certainly an understatement about the animal which would soon become the most famous canine in Italy and, possibly, the entire world.

The jewelry store that had been burglarized during the night was located in the center of Turin. The robbery was discovered by the owner, who had come to the store early in the morning in order to take inventory. The inventory was sadly incomplete. A number of costly rings, bracelets, necklaces, and watches were missing. The investigating officers who had initially arrived on the scene found no clue except a workman's glove, covered with grease and dirt. It was an interesting piece of evidence, but at that time it could not be linked up with any other elements to aid in the investigation.

The detectives were trying to obtain additional evidence when Officer Maimone and his dog entered the jewelry store. One of the men turned to Maimone and asked good-naturedly: "Do you think, Giovanni, Dox can lend us a paw?" The man and his dog were well known and well liked in the department. But Dox was still considered a pet—not a police dog.

Maimone answered cheerfully, "From what I understand you fellows aren't doing so well. Who knows, maybe Dox can show you a thing or two."

The owner of the jewelry store listened to this banter disgustedly.

Giovanni Maimone, as he confessed later, was not as cheerful as he pretended to be. After all, this was his dog's first assignment and a great deal would depend on the outcome. The officer was convinced that dogs could play an important role in law enforcement, but at that time very few of his colleagues took him seriously.

Maimone addressed the detective in charge. "I understand you found a glove that may belong to one of the suspects."

"Yes. It's here in this paper bag," answered the detective. "Help yourself, but don't lose it."

Maimone took the glove from the paper bag and held it in front of Dox. The animal had been standing quietly near the door, his big eyes watching the proceedings with obvious curiosity. Dox sniffed at the glove. Somehow Maimone knew that the dog understood what was expected of him. He had to select the scent belonging to the owner of the glove. This important piece of evidence had been handled by the owner of the jewelry store and some of the detectives. It was a pretty difficult task for a young police dog.

After ten seconds or so, Dox turned away from the glove and ran across the store, sniffing the floor. It did not take him long to find a corresponding smell. Dox went out of the store, followed by Maimone. Two other detectives were ordered to follow, for the decisive action of the animal aroused the men's curiosity. They recognized a definite pattern of progression in the dog's movements.

Dox slowly tracked for a few blocks until he reached an *autostrada* which led to an industrial section at the outskirts of town. There he stopped, and Maimone could sense that Dox had lost some of his decisiveness. But the officer left the dog alone.

Dox proceeded slowly and indecisively along the border of the highway, sometimes going a little faster, sometimes a little slower, and every once in a while retracing his steps.

After a mile or so the dog stopped. He looked around, trying to make up his mind what step to take next. Then, very slowly, he crossed a lane of the *strada* and made his way to a grass-covered divider.

Maimone and the two detectives followed every move of the dog as they joined him on the divider. The traffic was flowing by them in opposite directions. Dox, unexpectedly, let out a triumphal bark. Then he continued his tracking with the same assurance he had shown initially after leaving the jewelry store.

Maimone assumed that the dog had lost the scent on the *autostrada*. A multitude of interfering smells and especially the exhaust gases from cars must have made things difficult for the dog. It seemed that the suspect had proceeded in the same direction and somewhere had crossed over to the grass divider. There Dox found again the scent which was less contaminated by the passing traffic.

The dog continued on his way, straining on the leash. At an intersection he left the center divider, crossed one of the traffic lanes, and approached a street leading to a cluster of houses.

This was a very poor section of Turin. The houses were occupied by unskilled laborers, many of them out of work. The region was well familiar to the officers of the Turin police force; many of the people living there had been in trouble with the law.

Dox, his nose so close to the ground that it almost touched, went straight to one of the houses. Officer Maimone, who wanted to make his own approach as inconspicuous as possible, released the dog from the leash. Dox ran straight to one of the buildings, jumped over a wooden fence, and placed himself in front of a door. Then he turned back to see whether his entourage was following.

Maimone opened the gate and the officer and the two detectives crossed over to the door. The dog was again fastened to the leash by his master. One of the detectives knocked.

After a short while a middle-aged woman opened the door. She was clad in a sleazy robe and carried a baby. She looked suspiciously at the men and at the dog. The way Dox could smell criminals, she could smell the police.

"What is it you want?" she asked.

The police officers identified themselves and while one of the detectives started interrogating the woman, Dox pulled Maimone into the house. The officer followed the dog with an apologetic look at the woman who did not seem to care. The objective of the dog was a chair in the kitchen. He pulled over to it and smelled it with concentration. Then he growled at the chair and sat down next to it. He turned to Maimone as if to say, "This is it! Now it's your turn to get some action."

The detective, in the meantime, had discovered that the name of the woman was Maria Martinelli, wife of Guido Martinelli. The officer had watched the dog's action from the corner of his eyes. It gave him ample reason to thoroughly question the woman.

"Where is your husband, signora?" he asked the woman, who did not seem to be very shaken by the sudden appearance of the police.

"In jail," Signora Martinelli answered matter-of-factly.

"Since when?" continued the detective.

"Since two months," continued the woman. "He has six more months to go."

"What is he in for?" the detective wanted to know.

"Burglary," said the woman. "And he was framed."

"Naturally," answered the detective. "They all are framed." After a pause he continued: "Are there any other men living here?"

"No, I'm alone—except for my little son Franco," she answered, pointing to her baby.

The detectives asked the signora's permission to search the premises. The woman had no choice but to consent. Every room and every possible hiding place was systematically searched but nothing of interest could be turned up. The men decided to go back to town, for Guido Martinelli could not have committed the robbery while in jail.

Dox did not want to leave the place. He still growled at the chair in the kitchen but the two detectives and his master looked at him admonishingly. Had he led them on a wild goose chase ...? Giovanni Maimone, at that time, did not have the complete confidence in the dog's judgment he was to gain in the next few years.

Upon returning to police headquarters the detectives checked the woman's story in a routine manner. They were in for a surprise. The name Guido Martinelli was well represented in the police files and, indeed, the man had a long list of robberies and some convictions on his record. He had served many months in jail. But right now he was free.

The detectives rushed back to the house of Maria Martinelli, but the woman stuck to her story. Her husband was in jail, or at least was supposed to be.

In the meantime the crime lab went into action. The men compared certain particles of dirt that adhered to the glove found in the jewelry store with dirt particles collected in the Martinelli home. It could be established without any doubt that this glove had been in both locations—hence a man living in the Martinelli house must be the burglar.

Equipped with this additional information it was not difficult to obtain a confession from Maria Martinelli. She admitted that she was lying to the police in order to give her husband a little more time to escape into the country. Guido Martinelli had taken all the loot from the jewelry store with him and hoped to be able to dispose of it. But two days later the suspect was tracked down and arrested. His wife was a liar no longer. Her husband was indeed in jail.

Dox received his first official acknowledgement for having taken part in a police action and for having been responsible for a speedy solution. He made his first headline in Turin's daily newspaper *Tempo*.

It was not long before Dox produced additional material for the editors of the Italian press. The general public became aware of the dog and the editors became aware of the great reader interest in the dog's adventures. "Dox" stories wandered from the back pages to the front page of the newspapers and the picture of the long-haired German shepherd became a well-known attraction to Italian readers. A readership study was conducted by the Italian newspaper *El Paese* on a day it reported an arrest for which Dox was responsible. The "Dox" story was read by more persons than any other news item printed that day.

After a round of duty in Turin and in Sicily, Giovanni Maimone, then Sergeant Maimone, joined the police force of Rome in 1958 for service with the Squadra Mobile. Dox and his master were assigned to quarters on the top floor of the Squadra Mobile building located on the left bank of the Tiber. Dox's favorite resting place was near a window that faced the famous river and it seemed that the dog took in the entire panorama of smells from the eternal city.

By that time the capabilities of this great animal were fully recognized all over Italy and well appreciated by the law enforcement personnel. Trips to foreign countries brought the dog's talents to the attention of admiring police officers outside Italy.

As far as the Roman Police were concerned, Dox ceased to be considered a dog. He was looked upon as a full-fledged detective, well liked and well respected by most and a puzzle to all. The way the human race produces its share of mental giants, the canine species every so often brings forth an animal of unusual talents—the one in a million.

The super-canine reasoning powers of Dox can be recognized in the following story. The case occurred when

the dog and Maimone were on duty with the Squadra
Mobile in Rome.

It was another jewelry store robbery. Only this time
Maimone did not have to ask for permission to be assigned to the case with his dog. He and Dox were "invited" to join in the investigation.

Roman Police Headquarters had received a call from
a night watchman who worked for a number of mer-
chants. The man reported the robbery of the jewelry
store, which he had discovered while on his rounds. A
squad of detectives was dispatched immediately to investigate the crime.

Sergeant Maimone took his special car and he and Dox
arrived at the robbed jewelry store a few minutes after
the first contingent of detectives got there. An orientation
by the officers and the night watchman revealed that the
burglar had blasted his way into the jewelry store from
the cellar of the adjoining building.

"Did you get a good look at the robber?" Maimone
asked the night watchman.

"Unfortunately not, Sergeant. He kicked my flashlight
out of my hands and we fought in the dark."

Maimone turned to his colleagues from the Squadra
Mobile. "Did you locate anything of interest?"

"Nothing so far," was the unanimous answer.

Maimone stepped over to Dox, who had been sitting
quietly in a corner. He knew his turn for action would be
coming soon. "Come on, boy, see what you can do," he
was told by his master. By that time Maimone's commands for Dox had assumed a rather informal conversa-
tional character in place of the initially used sharp
commands.

Dox did not need much encouragement. His scent discrimination was at its peak. His instinct to select the key
scent from a number of cross-scents was beyond compre-

hension. The dog started tracking immediately. He knew exactly what was expected of him; his bearing was that of a professional.

The dog crawled through the hole the burglar had chipped through the wall and jumped into the cellar of the adjoining building. Maimone and two other detectives followed with considerably less agility. As expected, Dox made his way along the corridor of the basement, then up a stairway and into the street. There was little pedestrian and vehicular traffic at this early time when night had just made way for dawn. The dog, followed by the men, could proceed at a brisk pace along what seemed to be a comparatively fresh track. One of the detectives followed in a Squadra Mobile vehicle.

The group progressed along a route developing in a pattern well familiar to the investigators. The burglaries were usually committed in one of the luxurious sections of the city. The criminal's track led to the poor districts of Rome.

Dox finally stopped in front of an old, dilapidated house that was located at the bottom of a hill. Maimone tried the front door and found that it was not locked. He opened the front door and Dox slipped in quickly. The officers' flashlights revealed a narrow corridor, smelling of bad food and poverty.

Dox ran swiftly through the corridor toward a stairway. The dog and the men descended. There were a number of doors leading to coal bins, storage and utility rooms. Dox stopped in front of one of them, scratching on it with his powerful paws.

Maimone knocked; there was no answer. The man tried to turn the handle but the door was locked. Dox sniffed and then he scratched again as if to say, "There is somebody inside."

His master knocked again, this time more powerfully.

"Leave me alone," said a male voice from inside the room.

"Open up! Police!" said Maimone with authority.

"Who?" answered the voice.

"Police!" repeated Maimone. "And make it quick!"

The men waited with their guns drawn. Maimone was not worried about his safety. His personal guard was fully alert; crouched against the floor, tensed to jump into action in case of need.

After a brief pause the men heard the shuffle of bare-foot steps. The door opened. The beams of the flashlights hit a medium-sized man, clad in a dirty shirt and a pair of dirty trousers. One of the detectives recognized the suspect immediately. The man had committed a number of burglaries and had served time in jail. Dox growled at the man and then looked back to his handler. The dog's expression indicated as clearly as can be: "That's him!"

"We meet again, Ceasare Zoglio," said the detective who had recognized the suspect.

"But now I am clean, signori; I'm going straight." The suspect explained that he was the janitor of this building and in this capacity making an honest living.

"Then tell us, Ceasare, what have you been doing last night and this morning?" one of the detectives wanted to know. The suspect seemed to be delighted to explain:

"I can prove I was right here all night. I came here with a friend, Luigi Patino—and he will tell you so— around ten in the evening." Zoglio pointed at a number of empty bottles on the floor. "Luigi and I drank a few bottles of wine. My friend left and I fell asleep. I slept until you men disturbed me . . ."

Ceasare Zoglio's behavior was very convincing, and the detectives were inclined to give some credence to his story. But there was Dox to reckon with, who had fol-lowed the conversation with his alert eyes, seemingly un-derstanding every single word.

"Come with us, then," said Sergeant Maimone to the suspect. "I would like somebody to see you. Your guilt or innocence can be easily established." Maimone figured that the night watchman would be able to tell whether or not Zoglio was the burglar of the jewelry store.

"I'm so sleepy, signori, such a headache. Not now."

"We will take you by car," said one of the detectives. "You'll be back very soon. If you're innocent you have nothing to fear."

"*Bene,*" said Zoglio, knowing that he had no choice. "I'll be going with you just to get it over with."

The group left the shabby quarters of the suspect and stepped into the waiting police car. Dox was the last to jump in. In a few minutes they were back at the jewelry store.

The detectives asked the night watchman to take a good look at the suspect and to talk to him for a while. But the guard could not make up his mind.

"I can't say this was the man," the guard said. "There is nothing about him that reminds me of the burglar. Also, the man I fought was much taller and stronger."

Sergeant Maimone listened with interest. He knew from experience that criminals who escape from police officers or night watchmen usually seem to gain a few inches in height and a good number of pounds in weight.

Maimone and two of the detectives stepped aside to discuss the case. They knew that they did not have enough evidence to arrest the man without a positive identification from the night watchman. The action of the dog, while interesting, would never stand up in court. Dogs are not considered reliable witnesses, not even a canine with the reputation of Dox.

"Dox could have made a mistake," said the detective who recognized the suspect.

"Never made one so far," countered Maimone. "But I

see your point. Any attorney could get his client off under those circumstances."

In the meantime the fingerprint experts from the crime lab had gone over the place. No prints were determined that could be associated with the suspect. Anyhow, an interrogation with the night watchman indicated that the burglar had worn gloves as any experienced one would.

Ceasare Zoglio relaxed. Dox, who knew exactly what was going on, became increasingly restless. He passed by the suspect and growled and paced through the jewelry store.

"All right, Ceasare," said one of the detectives. "We will take you back home in a minute."

The suspect beamed with delight.

At that instant the dog's ears went up and Dox moved over to the rubble that was smashed in the store by the blast. Dox started digging, looking every once in a while over his shoulders at his master.

"What is he trying to do?" asked one of the detectives.

"I've no idea," confessed Maimone. "But let's give him all the time he wants."

Ceasare Zoglio, who was just as puzzled by the dog's action as everybody else, felt it was time to leave. "You said you'll take me home," he addressed one of the detectives. "I could walk, I don't mind; I'm wide awake now." Zoglio indicated that he would leave.

"You stay, until we tell you to go," said the officer who guarded him.

Dox continued to dig and search in the rubble. After a few minutes he let out a little bark and dug up a small object with his teeth. He carried it over to his master, who noticed that it was a button. Then Dox turned away and left the store again, loping back along the route he had taken earlier. Maimone and the other detectives followed with the suspect in the police car. Dox entered

Zoglio's cellar, sniffed at a closet along the wall, and nudged open the door. A wornout raincoat was hanging inside. Dox pulled it out gently with his mouth and walked over to his master. As Maimone took it, Dox nosed a spot on the coat where hanging threads indicated a missing button. The sergeant held the button in his pocket up to one of the buttons on the raincoat, and they matched.

Sergeant Maimone turned to the suspect and showed him the two pieces of evidence. "Now, what do you have to say?"

Ceasare Zoglio cast a vitriolic look at Dox, realizing there was nothing to be accomplished by denying his guilt. He confessed that he had broken into the jewelry store.

Giovanni Maimone and Dox left the cellar just as the first rays of sunshine flooded over the eternal city. They drove back to their quarters. For them it had been just another job.

Sergeant Giovanni Maimone and his dog Dox served with the Squadra Mobile until late 1962. Their separation from the Force was, unfortunately, an anticlimax to a fascinating career. Due to a string of unfortunate circumstances created by some minor government officials, the services of the famous man-dog team of the Squadra Mobile were terminated in a rather undignified manner. Giovanni Maimone and Dox had to vacate their quarters suddenly in one day.

The "Dox Case" constituted a bureaucratic blunder of the first order and the Italian public was enraged. And if the citizens of Italy get angry something has got to give. True, Dox was at that time seventeen years old and not as active as he used to be. According to human standards the dog was over one hundred years old. But, as it was pointed out eagerly, the entire life of the dog was so exceptional that ordinary norms could not be applied. Also, as the police department readily admitted, Dox was still called in on unusual cases which could not be entrusted to ordinary police dogs. It was hoped, further, that Dox would become the patriarch of a dynasty of great police dogs.

The animal's forced and sudden retirement prompted a flood of angry protest from all the news media which triggered a furious reaction on the part of the citizens. Pictures in newspapers, magazines, and television showed the "evicted" police dog champion lying on a dirty sidewalk during the cold November night. And Dox managed to look very crestfallen. Dox's fate was shared by his master and the dog's two offsprings—Dox, Jr. and the young Kira.

As the controversy fed on its own momentum, hundreds of invitations were extended to Giovanni Maimone offering hospitality for the man and his dogs.

Sergeant Maimone and his canine family finally accepted the hospitality of an Italian movie actor. The disenchanted handler resigned from the Squadra Mobile in order to continue the care and training of his dogs.

An investigation was ordered by the Minister of Justice to determine the responsibility for the bad judgment that was used in the dismissal of the most popular dog in Italy. It turned out that a minor official in the Finance Bureau had started a ball of red tape rolling. Nobody was able to stop it or to cut it. Apologies were made to Giovanni Maimone and the dog expert agreed to continue some of his activities in connection with the training of police dogs.

Dox reached the age of nineteen years, one month and seven days—a record for a German shepherd. He died on June 11, 1965.

The dog that shows greatest promise in this new generation in the Canine Corps is Dox, Jr. Whether or not he will reach the champion's reputation is still conjecture, but Dox, Jr. is already working with the Roman Police Force and rapidly building up an excellent service record.

3

A Story from France

Some of the French law enforcement agencies have employed supporting canine units for a good number of years. The Paris Police has a small though effective dog squad. The Direction Generale de la Gendarmerie Nationale, which is comparable to the state troopers in the United States, instituted a systematic police dog development program after World War II.

The dogs are prepared for their duties in a special school located in the Corrèze District in the center of France. More than other countries, France attempted to utilize a number of breeds for police work. It was again the German shepherd who showed the best *savoir-faire* and today, practically all French police dogs belong to that breed.

The canine units of France are already credited with numerous astounding deeds. One of the reports stands

out because of the unique pattern of search stemming
from the criminal's action. The talents of a dog and his
master made it possible to achieve the speedy solution
of a crime which was, as the French would say, rather
"bizarre."

Gendarme Auguste Pellier was sitting at his desk in
the little town of Barrancourt. It was a brilliant summer
day in 1958, and the villagers had settled down to a
leisurely lunch.

Glancing through the window, Pellier could see his dog
"Droll," a sleek German shepherd, who had been his
steady companion for almost a year. Pellier had great
affection for the dog who, he said, was a useful gendarme
at work and a good partner in times of rest.

Droll had assumed his favorite vantage point, the
stairs in front of the gendarmerie from where he could
overlook the village square. There seemed no doubt in
Droll's mind that this square was his private domain and
that his very presence there would keep everyone out of
trouble.

Gendarme Pellier cut a slice of bread from a two-foot
long loaf. Cheese and a bottle of wine would make a
tasty lunch. He was just about to take the first bite when
the telephone rang.

"Sacre bleu!" he mumbled to himself. "They always
wait until I get ready to eat." He picked up the receiver.

"Gendarmerie Barrancourt," Pellier said with a voice
of authority.

"This is Emile Lavarlard," said the voice on the other
end of the line.

Emile Lavarlard, Pellier knew, had a farm in his district.

"Bonjour, Monsieur," continued the gendarme politely.
"What can I do for you?"

"Somebody entered my house this morning and took

off with all my savings," said Lavarlard with a distraught voice.

"How much was taken?" asked Pellier with concern.

"About 45,000 francs. All the money I had."

Pellier cast a sad look at his bread, cheese, and wine and said, "I'll be at your place in a short while. Don't touch anything until I get there!"

"*Merci beaucoup, merci beaucoup,*" answerd Lavarlard. Pellier replaced the receiver and then dialed the inn across the square. He had to ask his deputy to interrupt his lunch and to come back to the post.

The policeman wrapped his lunch into a newspaper, put on his belt with the revolver, and grabbed his cap. A brief look in the mirror convinced him that he looked very much the law-enforcer. Also, through the mirror, he saw his canine partner wagging his tail in excited anticipation.

"*Allons!*" said Pellier as he and the dog descended the stairs of the gendarmerie and walked over to his small Citröen. He held the door open for the dog, who eased into the car without difficulty. Then, with less agility, Pellier took his seat behind the wheel.

The gendarme drove off, thinking of the problem on hand. He had known Emile Lavarlard and his wife Marie for years. Their farm was located about fifteen kilometers from the village. Lavarlard managed to make a modest living from the few acres he owned and most of his earnings were used to give his children as good an education as circumstances permitted. There was a son, Michel, about seventeen, who helped his parents in the fields. And there were two additional youngsters, a girl and a boy, attending the village school. The Lavarlards had owned their land for generations as did the peasants who had farms nearby. It was unthinkable that any of Lavarlard's neighbors would have committed the crime.

"Must've been an outsider," mused the gendarme barely

avoiding a flock of chickens crossing the street. Droll
barked at them fiercely; he considered them a very in-
ferior form of life.

"Why don't these French peasants put their money
into a bank?" Pellier said to Droll. "They still believe in
the safety of the mattress and other obvious hiding
places . . ." Then he smiled to himself. Was he more
sophisticated? His money, whatever there was, was hidden safely below one of the floorboards in his bedroom.
"Who knows about banks anyway . . . ?"

Pellier slowed down his car as he approached the
modest farmhouse belonging to the Lavarlards. He
turned into the path leading to the house, a path acquainted better with the iron-rimmed wheels of horse-
drawn carts than the tires of the Citröen.

The arrival of the automobile brought Monsieur and
Madame Lavarlard out of the house, closely followed by
their son, Michel. Pellier stepped out of his car and
ordered his dog to stay put—*"Reste ici!"* The dog obeyed,
a reluctant look in his eyes.

"Bonjour, Monsieur Pellier," said Emile Lavarlard.
"Thank you for coming so quickly."

"What an unfortunate occasion . . ." added Marie. The
gendarme could see that the woman had been crying.

Emile Lavarlard led the gendarme into the house and
guided him to the kitchen. He pointed to a metal box on
the cupboard.

"This morning it contained all my money. Now it is
empty."

Lavarlard then explained that this metal box was purposely placed among plates, cups, bottles of wine, dishes,
and other household paraphernalia in order to "camou-
flage" its mission. But, unfortunately, this place had not
been good enough.

Gendarme Pellier looked at the empty metal box and
then turned to Emile and Marie Lavarlard. "Now, my

friends, tell me exactly what you did this morning. Don't leave out anything."

The story was simple enough.

Emile and his son Michel had left the house at six thirty in the morning and walked to the far field. It was harvest time and they were busier than ever. In order to save time, Marie brought their lunch to the field. As she returned to the farmhouse about eleven she put a few utensils back in the cupboard. While doing so she noticed that the metal box was open. She grabbed it, found it was empty, and almost fainted. After recovering from the shock Marie rushed back to the far field and told her husband what had happened. Emile went to one of his neighbors who had a telephone and called the gendarmerie. That was about half an hour ago.

"Did any of you see a stranger around here?" asked Pellier.

"No, we did not see anybody or anything suspicious, nor did any of the neighbors we talked to."

The peasant and his wife looked at the gendarme expectantly. What action would he take?

The first action Pellier took was to whistle for his dog. Droll, who had been waiting impatiently for his master's voice, jumped from the car and was at Pellier's side in a second. The dog looked at his master, his eyes asking, "What am I supposed to do now?"

Pellier took the metal box from the cupboard and put it in front of the dog. Droll knew well what was expected of him. He sniffed at the box carefully. But probably because the box had been last handled by Emile and Marie Lavarlard, he turned first to them. The animal knew instinctively that these were not the people his master was after. The dog glanced at Pellier; their eyes conveyed a message of mutual understanding.

The dog took another long sniff at the box, then paced around the place, unable to make up his mind. Finally he came to a decision and started to track. Pellier knew his dog was up to something by the way Droll's hair bristled around his neck. Dog handlers—and other dog owners at that—can recognize certain reactions of their animals by physical manifestations. It may be the position of the ears, the general posture of the animal's body; everyone knows that a tail can reveal every shade of emotion.

Droll started on a track that led through the kitchen door into the yard behind the farmhouse. The dog went on, completely disregarding the chickens and their excited cackling. Pellier was following, and so were the Lavarlards, keeping a respectful distance.

Droll crossed the yard and made his way to a narrow opening in the fence surrounding the house. He went through this opening, tracked in a straight line across a field to the main road. There he stopped. As Pellier caught up with his dog he saw him sniffing all around. But Droll, surprisingly, seemed to have lost his trail. The dog backtracked a few feet but realized the futility of this action.

Pellier encouraged his dog to continue the tracking but to no avail. The gendarme then decided to follow a hunch and led the dog down the road in the direction of the village. He had Droll cross from left to right and from right to left in the hope that he might somehow come on the track again.

The plan worked. After some two hundred feet the dog suddenly stopped and carefully sniffed the ground. Then he lunged forward, practically dragging Pellier toward the gate leading into the front yard of a nearby house. There was a cluster of six houses in this vicinity.

As Droll arrived at the gate he stood still for a few seconds. Then he scratched at the door of the house. The owner, M. Coquelet, opened the door and looked somewhat surprised to see the dog, the gendarme, and the Lavarlards in the background. Pellier explained the reason for their presence and M. Coquelet willingly agreed to let the dog enter and do whatever he wanted. But Droll was not interested in entering the house. He sniffed the area in front of the door several times, turned around, and headed back toward the road.

Pellier knew that the person or persons they were after had not entered the house. He was sure that M. Coquelet would not be a suspect, for Droll would have shown it immediately; he was not a friendly dog when he caught up with his prey. Aside from that, the Lavarlards and the Coquelets were the best of friends.

Droll, in the meantime, again crossed the street and pulled Pellier to another house. The dog went through the same routine. He went as far as the threshold, sniffed the area, and turned back to the road. He was not interested in entering the premises nor in the occupants. Pellier began to wonder about the unprecedented antics of his dog. Was he affected by the day's heat?

"It's a beautiful dog," said Emile Lavarlard, "but what is he doing?" Marie Lavarlard, at this point, claimed fatigue and went back to her home. But her expression revealed disappointment rather than tiredness.

The gendarme and his dog continued their strange journey. There was nothing else they could do. And Droll repeated the identical procedure at the four remaining houses in that vicinity. When the dog turned from the sixth house back to the road he stopped. He sniffed in all directions and Pellier realized that Droll had lost his track. The gendarme and the dog, still followed by Emile Lavarlard, went down the road in the direction of the village. The dog, again, checked both sides of the road but to no avail. After they had walked a mile or so Pellier stopped the search.

Both man and dog were tired. Pellier spotted a bench and sat down. Droll made himself comfortable at his master's feet. It was four o'clock in the afternoon and

Pellier's stomach reminded him that he had skipped his lunch. Reaching into the pocket of his jacket, he retrieved a piece of chocolate, a sort of iron ration he kept there for emergencies such as this. There was also a piece of sugar for his dog.

While the man munched on his chocolate he was considering the perplexing action of his dog. It was a puzzling but consistent pattern. Therefore there had to be an explanation. The owners of all the houses they had approached had been thoroughly interrogated. Nothing was stolen from any of the houses. Nobody had spoken to or seen a stranger on that day. And the persons living there were all above reproach, even considering the professionally suspicious mind of a French gendarme. Pellier patted the head of his dog, an almost unconscious sign of affection. The dog had tried his best. What more can you ask?

Whenever Pellier and Droll made an appearance some of the people of the village gathered around them to talk to the man and to admire the dog. This day was no exception and Pellier did not mind it. As a matter of fact he encouraged conversation. Who knows—someone might provide a clue to the theft.

While they talked, one of the men noticed the postman approaching on his bicycle from the direction of the village and called to him to stop and join the group. He wanted to tell the postman about the theft and, of course, ask him whether he would have any information that might be helpful for Monsieur le Gendarme.

As the man on the bicycle drew nearer Droll's head tilted up, the hair around his neck bristling. As soon as the man dismounted, Droll bounced forward, barking furiously. Pellier who had, as was his habit, the sling of his dog's leash around the wrist of his left hand, was almost thrown off the bench.

Pellier finally managed to control the dog, who wanted

to attack the postman. Emile Lavarlard and the other villagers were amazed at this sudden outburst of fury. Pellier was not amazed but pleased. He decided to thoroughly question the target of Droll's ire. The post-man was escorted to the Lavarlard farm in spite of his vehement protests. Droll kept close to the suspect's heels as if waiting for him to make a wrong move. That, of course, did not enter the postman's mind. By the time they reached the farm Pellier had a pretty good theory of what had happened, a theory that would explain Droll's strange tracking pattern and should clear up the theft.

But, so far, it was just theory. It had to be corroborated by the suspect, and the postman was not about to in-criminate himself. The interrogation went into the sec-ond hour. Droll did not stop snarling at the man. Pellier could have quieted Droll with a short command but he felt that the behavior of the dog might add to the sus-pect's psychological strain.

Pellier's consistent questioning and Droll's ferocious barking eventually weakened the postman's resistance. He broke down and confessed to the theft of the 45,000 francs. What is more, the money was still in his wallet and he handed it to the gendarme.

Pellier looked at his watch. It was half-past seven in the evening and all was over.

The postman's story was as simple as Droll's tracking pattern was intricate. A few days ago the suspect had been invited by Mme. Lavarlard for a glass of wine and sat down for a brief rest in the kitchen. While enjoying this hospitality he saw the woman putting some money into the metal box in the cupboard. Then and there he decided to get this money.

This very morning when he passed by the Lavarlard farm on his bicycle to deliver the mail he had noticed Mme. Lavarlard leaving the house. She had a basket under her arm and he assumed that she went to bring food to her husband and son who were working in a field about a kilometer away.

The postman knew that he would have the place to himself for a while. He sneaked through an opening in the fence into the back yard of the farm and entered the kitchen. The door was open. He had no difficulty finding the metal box which, to his great joy, contained more money than he anticipated. He left the same way he entered—straight through the back yard and through the opening in the fence (Droll had picked up his track leading to this spot). Then he stepped on his bicycle (Droll lost his track) and drove down to M. Coquelet's house where he dismounted (and where Droll picked up his scent) to deliver the mail.

He continued delivering the mail to the other five houses in that area on foot (Droll followed his tracks from house to house). Having delivered all the letters at the last house, he again stepped on his bicycle and drove all the way to the village (and Droll lost his track for good).

Gendarme Auguste Pellier formally arrested the man and drove him to the gendarmerie station.

4

The Dogs
of the RCMP

In the years prior to 1935, Sergeant J. N. Cawsey of the Royal Canadian Mounted Police owned a German shepherd dog named Dale. Sergeant Cawsey, who was stationed in Alberta, was an ardent dog fancier and, in addition, possessed practical knowledge of training methods. Under his instruction Dale progressed well and assisted him materially on a number of investigations. As a result of Dale's successes, the RCMP became interested in dogs as law enforcement aid and purchased Dale from Sergeant Cawsey. Thus, in the year 1935, the Canadian Police Service Dog Section was born.

Progress was slow at the beginning and the Section did not show any appreciable development until about the middle forties. However, by 1947 the experiment was proving such a success that the Commissioner of the RCMP ordered a training school for dogs and masters to be organized at Calgary, Alberta.

In the beginning the Force was not too selective on the breed of dog accepted for training. Experiments were carried out with Rottweilers, Riesenschnauzers, and Doberman pinschers, as well as German shepherds. While all these dogs have certain qualities which suit them for police duties, it was again established that for RCMP purposes the German shepherd was the most suitable.

At the present time the RCMP is undertaking a breeding program at the Training Kennels at Innisfail, Alberta, which provides a reserve of trained Police Service Dogs when field replacements are required.

The Canadian police dogs and their masters work as teams and are stationed at key points from coast to coast throughout Canada. These teams are in readiness at all times of night or day to respond to requests for assistance in locating lost persons, lost or stolen articles, illicit spirits, evidence at scenes of crimes, in trailing criminals, and guarding prisoners or evidence. When not engaged in actual cases the dog master grooms, exercises, and works his dog each day on simulated cases, thereby maintaining the animal's interest and efficiency at a high level throughout its service.

Care is taken during these practice periods to keep the dog from becoming saturated or overtrained, which may cause him to become bored and disinterested while actually working on a case. Bearing this in mind, the exercises are normally terminated while the dog still displays good interest and has performed the particular exercise well.

Each year the dogs and masters are assembled at central points and participate in a short refresher course under the direction of a trainer. Simulated cases are worked by each team, thus providing the trainer with an opportunity to assess each team's ability and performance and correct any shortcomings. In addition, those persons who have expressed a desire to become dog masters and are thought to possess suitable qualifications, are de-tailed to act as quarries. In this capacity they lay trails, conceal articles, and act the part of a criminal.

The RCMP now has twenty-two dogs in the field. Their value in a country where one officer may police an area as large as the state of Massachusetts is acknowledged both by the officers and the civilians. The following case histories will show why.

A Day in the Life of "Sarj"

The tour of duty experienced by police dog Sarj from August 14 to 15, 1959, cannot be considered typical even for this amazing dog. Police work can be drab for many days and weeks and there is nothing to do for police dogs but to wait and to be prepared. Such a period pre-ceded this date in August. Then, everything happened at once. Within a period of twenty hours, Sarj and his handler were called upon to take part in three different investigations of entirely different nature.

In the afternoon of August 14, the personnel of the Arborg and Teulon Detachment, the dog Sarj, and his handler were combing the woods of the Sky Lane Dis-trict, in Manitoba, Winnipeg. They were engaged in a search for illicit spirits near the farm of Jack Leader. It was a frustrating case. The RCMP was sure that the man was engaged in the manufacture and sale of "moonshine" but they never succeeded in linking the evidence to the suspect. Leader's property had been searched a number of times in the past but without success.

Constable Hendrix of the Detachment concluded that

Leader's distilling equipment and the illicit spirits would be hidden somewhere off the suspect's property.

The constable's theory proved to be correct. The men followed a brush trail northeast from the farm buildings. Hendrix noticed a bunch of dead tree branches on the ground which did not look quite natural. He pushed them aside with his boot and saw that they were covering an excavation. It did not take the men long to uncover four barrels, each containing forty-five gallons of wash.

But there was a hitch to it. This cache was on the other side of a fence and a few hundred yards away from Leader's property. Nothing further could be found on the suspect's land and, as it might well be expected, Leader denied having any knowledge of the wash.

It was late afternoon. The investigators were ready to call it a day. They had combed the entire farm but Leader seemed to be too smart to get caught.

The dog master, who was a systematic man, pointed to a patch of brush across an east-west municipal road running to the south of Leader's property.

"That's the only place we haven't searched so far," he said to the other officers. "Why don't Sarj and I go across for a quick look. You stay here and rest."

The dog master and Sarj took off. Upon reaching the area Sarj began running around a dense bush. The dog became increasingly excited and indicated that he had located something. Sarj and the other men who were called over to help worked their way to the thick center of the bush, where the dog found three full gallons of "home brew." He continued his search with greater confidence, and soon located an additional three gallons in three separate caches.

The evidence, located by the Police Service Dog, was examined. One of the containers yielded a good set of fingerprints. When Jack Leader was confronted with the new evidence he confessed, adding some hateful remarks about dogs in general and Sarj in particular.

But Sarj and his handler were already on their way home. Both were tired from walking all day through the woods.

At five o'clock the next morning (August 15), the telephone rang. The Headingly Department was on the line asking for Hendrix and his dog.

"We have a breaking, entering, and theft at the Manitoba Pool Elevator. Happened during the night. Could you come with your dog?"

An hour later Hendrix arrived on the scene. The other investigators filled him in. In their opinion the offense was the work of local juveniles, because the articles stolen from the elevator were oranges, a large can of fruit juice, a pocket knife, and, most important, a set of keys removed from the trousers of the foreman. Great concern was felt about these keys as they would make possible the entry to any Manitoba pool elevator in the province. In the wrong hands the result could be disastrous.

The sergeant from the Headingly post said to Hendrix, "If local juveniles had taken the keys they may not know their value. So, who knows, they might have thrown them away somewhere in this area—and that's where Sarj comes in."

The dog looked up at the man with understanding eyes. Hendrix started a systematic search of the land surrounding the elevator. "Walking again," Hendrix muttered. Sarj did not seem to mind. He liked this exercise. His one wish was obviously to find whatever the humans seemed to be looking for. Hendrix and Sarj walked in ever-increasing circles around the elevator. An hour and a half after the search began, the team arrived at a drainage ditch. It was dry and its bottom was covered with a thick growth of grass sprouting high in the summer sun.

Hendrix sat down at the edge of the ditch. "Go—look!" he ordered the dog.

Sarj understood. He jumped into the ditch, forcing his way through the high grass in a tank-like fashion. Hendrix, enjoying the morning sun, watched the movements of the dog, so powerful and still so graceful.

Suddenly, there was a one-beat bark. Hendrix looked up. Sarj was racing toward him. When the dog reached his master he stood still, his right front paw a few inches from the ground, head slightly tilted to the right. He gave another bark.

Hendrix knew that the German shepherd had found something. He got up and followed Sarj's excited lead. Then the dog stopped. A few more barks asked, "Is this what you are looking for?".

It certainly was. There was a plastic bag full of oranges, an empty fruit juice can, and, most important of all, a set of keys.

Futher investigation failed to reveal the culprits, but there was no doubt that Sarj's recovery of the grain elevator keys was the most important part of the case. And it was all done within ninety minutes of tracking.

The members of the Headingly Detachment, the Winnipeg C.I.D., Identification Branch, Hendrix, and the dog Sarj drove to a cafe in Headingly for a delayed breakfast. The men were relaxing over a hot cup of coffee when the door burst open and another officer from the Detachment entered the room.

"Jail break!" the officer announced. "Just a few minutes ago. Three men got out."

Sarj was the first to get up. The coffee break ended abruptly and roadblocks were set up at strategic points in the area. The three inmates had broken out of the Headingly Provincial Jail, located three miles west of the town along the north bank of the Assiniboine River.

A member of the Headingly Detachment, Police Service Dog Sarj, and his master went to interview the persons who had reported the break. They were occupants of a dwelling just east of the jail.

The witnesses told the officers what had taken place about ten minutes earlier. Three persons had been seen running from the general direction of the prison and heading toward the dense bush along the north bank of the river. The fugitives wore prison clothes.

"Exactly where was it that you saw the men last?"

Hendrix put the question to the group surrounding the officers. One woman stepped forward and pointed to a small elevation across a field. "Right there. They were running in the direction of the Howard farm."

The Headingly officer turned to Hendrix. "Chances are they turned left or right. There are just open fields if they had continued straight on and they have to cross the river."

"Let's see whether Sarj can pick up their track," said the dog master. He started to walk the dog to the area that must have been crossed by the fugitives. Traversing their path at a right angle might put Sarj in tracking condition.

After a few mintues, Sarj indeed indicated fresh scent and followed it in an easterly direction through the dense bush. They reached the river, and the dog, without hesitation, turned right and continued eagerly for a few hundred yards. Clear fresh scent must be a dog's delight, and Sarj practically dragged his handler for the next few minutes.

A group of abandoned buildings put Hendrix and the Headingly officer on alert. Sarj was heading toward the nearest structure. Hendrix ordered "Halt!" The dog stopped, looking back at his master questioningly. His scent told him that the persons he was tracking could not be far away. So why stop?

At this very moment Sarj tensed, his front legs forward, belly touching the ground. A fraction of a second later a man jumped out of the window of the adjoining building and made off in an easterly direction into the bush.

A chase ensued; Sarj was still on the leash.

Brief glimpses were caught of the man in the bush. It was not possible to identify the fugitive as an inmate from the jail until the trail passed through a small clearing. The handler reached for his service revolver and fired a warning shot in the air. "Stop!" he ordered.

However, the shot only had the effect of speeding up the escapee. Sarj was turned loose.

"Attack!" ordered Hendrix and Sarj catapulted after the fugitive. The dog had approximately two hundred yards to cover before making contact with the man, and the gap was being closed rapidly.

The man, wondering about his progress, turned his head. It was then that he noticed the ninety-five pound German shepherd bearing down on him. It was a sobering sight, and the fugitive stopped in his tracks. Sarj, upon an order from the dog master, slowed down. Remembering his training, the dog did not press the attack any further. He ran around his prey, barking ferociously.

The fugitive seemed almost glad to be taken in custody by the constable. He was returned to the Headingly jail, uninjured physically but badly shaken mentally.

One down, two to go. Hendrix assumed that the three had split up when they saw the officers approach the abandoned building and had fled in different directions.

The guess was correct. What Hendrix did not anticipate, however, was that the two other escapees had made made their way right back to jail. The sight of their friend trapped by a dog was too much for them.

"We knew then," said one of them, "that this dog would've caught us sooner or later. Why wait?"

The only secure place they could think of was the jail. The dog would not follow them in there.

Hendrix looked at his watch, then at the dog Sarj. It

was just twenty hours since they had started their search for moonshine on Jack Leader's farm. Hendrix had certainly earned his money and Sarj his keep.

Two tired members of the Police Dog Service Section returned to the kennel.

"Silver"

Organized Canine Corps, whether they belong to a law enforcement unit or to the armed forces, use male dogs only. There are a number of reasons. Males are usually a little stronger than female dogs. "Mixed" kennels may produce rivalries and tensions among the males. Last but not least, females put themselves temporarily out of action before and after throwing a litter.

The following case history involving Silver is remarkable for a number of reasons. Silver is a female German shepherd. This much publicized dog was also the first in the history of the Canadian Dog Section to receive an official reward for outstanding services. Her handler, Constable Sanderson, and Silver were the most famous dog-man team in the RCMP. Their service in the force included a lengthy stretch in the Maritime Provinces prior to her transfer to British Columbia.

In the fall of 1954, the city of Vancouver experienced the worst crime wave in its history, and similar outbreaks occurred in the neighboring areas of New Westminster and West Vancouver. Among the crimes of violence, armed robbery predominated. In Vancouver, within a four-week period, there were five bank holdups, while two in New Westminster and another in West Vancouver brought the total to eight—with more than sixty-seven thousand dollars stolen by the bandits who made successful getaways.

This lawlessness was met by accelerated police vigilance. Municipal police forces were aided by the federal force, and these measures began to show results by mid-December. The bank robberies had ceased and other major crimes had been reduced in proportion.

In Burnaby, near Vancouver, a municipality of eighty thousand people policed by the RCMP, there had been no bank robberies for several years. However, the local Detachment had been reinforced by personnel from other points and extra vigilance was maintained into the month of January, when urgent police requirements elsewhere caused some of the extra strength to withdraw.

This was the situation on January 13, when the Royal Bank of Canada in Burnaby was held up by three armed and masked bandits, who cowed the staff of twenty-five, and three customers. Then they scooped up approximately twenty-seven thousand dollars and made their escape. Their entrance into the bank had been witnessed by a municipal employee who had dashed into the nearby post office and told the clerk to phone the police. In addition, the bank manager and an accountant also sounded the alarm, which was immediately flashed from the British Columbia Telegraph Company in Vancouver to the Radio Center of the Vancouver City Police.

The Burnaby RCMP had a receiver tuned to the Vancouver Police calls, and the Mounted Police operator picked up the Vancouver dispatcher advising of the bank holdup. The information was quickly relayed to the RCMP patrol cars then in service in Burnaby. The first car to respond was eight blocks away from the bank when it picked up the message, and it was followed immediately by a second car which had pulled up behind it.

Seconds later they were at the bank where eager citizens gave the constables the license number and description of the bandits' car. Other eye-witnesses indicated the direction taken by the desperados and the police cars took up the pursuit.

About two miles to the north a third police car had heard the call and with siren wailing was already on his way south over the route taken by the bandits' car. The officer in this car had noted an automobile approaching with high speed from the opposite direction which soon passed by him. The constable braked sharply to make a U-turn and was joined at that moment by other police cars.

Less than a mile from the bank the road curved west and then north again in an "S" pattern. The police saw the speeding car ahead manage the first part of the turn, but go into a dangerous skid toward the end of the curve. The driver of the bandits' car lost control of the vehicle, and it ended up in the ditch. Two of the occupants got out and stood beside it, pulling the hoods off their heads. The third disappeared in the bush.

The officers called on the holdup men to surrender. But, even though faced by armed and determined constables, the bandits tried to break away toward a narrow side road which offered some concealment. A few shots were fired by the constables and soon one of the bandits was captured with a bullet in his leg.

In the meantime, Police Service Dog Silver and her master were coming from Cloverdale, twenty-three miles away, and other reinforcements from nearby detachments and Vancouver City Police were converging on the scene. Soon the area was practically fenced in by police and patrol cars.

The second of the three bandits succeeded in making his way back to the road about a third of a mile from the place where he had abandoned the getaway car. He approached a man standing at his parked car and tried to intimidate him into giving it up. But within seconds one of the police cars arrived and arrested the criminal. Two of the three bank robbers were now in custody.

In the bandits' wrecked car the police found a canvas

sack containing over nine thousand dollars, along with a sawed-off shotgun and a .32 automatic. Nearby were the discarded hoods of the robbers.

One hour after the holdup, the police party from Cloverdale, including Silver, arrived at the scene. The handler took his dog to a point where a recently discarded overcoat had been located. Silver picked up a scent at once and trotted off through the bush. Numerous police officers equipped with walkie-talkies also entered the undergrowth at different points.

Silver made good progress and, after travelling a few hundred yards, paused at the base of an old stump where the police found a partly buried plastic bag containing almost fifteen thousand dollars. A second automatic was also found at the same spot.

The dog and her master pressed on, crossed the road, and re-entered the bush on the opposite side. Silver paused for a moment, found her bearings again and resumed the trail. For almost a mile she led her party through tangled bush. At times the trail changed direction as it neared roads, and at one point the dog dropped her head to the ground and paused momentarily. When the police investigated this new cause of her interest they found another two thousand dollars in cash. Smaller amounts of money were retrieved at other points along the trail.

Eventually the dog and her party emerged on the highway and a local citizen hurried over to relay the news that a stranger had run across the road and then into the bush. Obviously Silver was close behind the fugitive.

With police patrols closing in on all sides the trail had now led into a good strategic location. Ahead lay a creek too wide and too deep to ford, and on either side were residential areas. One police party drove north into the bush on the banks of the creek, while a second moved in from the east side.

The dog led her party straight north. Within a few minutes the detail moving east encountered a stranger. His explanation for his presence there was a lame one. He was placed under arrest and was on his way to the cells when Silver completed her tracking to the bank of the creek. Subsequently this man and the second one caught admitted their guilt. The wounded man elected trial by high court.

The entire chase was over in less than two hours after the bank robbery was committed. All the stolen money except ninety-eight dollars had been recovered, thanks largely to Silver's keen nose.

There were many satisfactory factors involved in the success of this case, including the valuable assistance and courage of unarmed citizens who had faced grave danger in confronting the bandits, excellent cooperation between different police departments, and the efficient use of all law-enforcement facilities.

However, grateful bank officials seemed to feel that one personality involved deserved special recognition, and on February 24, at a special presentation ceremony, Silver was given a handsome dog collar complete with a silver plate on which was inscribed:

"Presented to Silver for outstanding service
January 13, 1955. The Royal Bank of Canada."

5

Hobo Adopts a Family

The use of trained police dogs was pioneered in Europe, especially in England, and in Canada. Now, many communities in the United States, small and large, are becoming accustomed to the sight of a police officer performing his duties with the cooperation of a canine partner. In some instances the dog drives along in a squad car, and in other cases the dog walks along on his master's beat.

When not "on guard," most German shepherds offer a picture of tranquility and kindness. A nod of praise from his master and the dog's tail beats in a lively metronome-like allegro. But when in danger or feeling ill-at-ease, the German shepherd may betray his lupine ancestry. The tail moves under the belly, the ears go back, the lips are curled up, and sharp teeth are bared.

More often than not, it is this sight of the ferocious

beast that is offered to the dog's future human family at the first encounter. For it is the policy of most police departments in the United States to have the dog live with his master. At the time of his introduction to "his" family, the dog is a mature, fully-developed animal, with eighty to a hundred pounds of muscle and threatening poses; a picture of potential danger.

Even though the dog is fully trained at that time and under complete control by his master, precautions have to be taken to avoid an accident.

The dog handlers themselves are usually volunteers from the police ranks. Many of them have had previous experience with animals, such as service with one of the dog units of the armed forces. All of them have one thing in common, their love for dogs. Applicants are interrogated by a board of examiners who determine whether or not the officers are temperamentally suited to work in the Canine Corps. Dogs, generally, reflect many of the characteristics of their masters. This is especially important in police work, and steady, composed, easygoing men are given the preference.

Future police dogs are acquired from various sources. Some are bought from outstanding breeders; others are donated to police departments by citizens who want to make a contribution to the community or who, for reasons beyond their control, have to give up their pets. Surprisingly enough, the city pound is another good source of supply for some splendid animals.

First the dog is turned over to the police kennel. Then his human partner is selected. The two are given some time to find out how they are getting along with each other. The man and the dog then attend a special training school. It may be a police department unit or, in smaller communities, a kennel. After a course that may take about three months, the police officer and his canine partner emerge as a team.

Preparations begin to move the dog from the kennel, to which he is now thoroughly accustomed, into his master's home. In some areas, all the adult members of the household have to give their written consent to have the dog move in with them. More often than not, the same approval is requested from the immediate neighbors. Every community has its share of professional dog haters who may conceivably cause trouble after one of those "monsters" puts in an appearance. Inasmuch as the community has to make a considerable investment in the development of a man-dog team, estimated to be in the neighborhood of two thousand dollars, any antagonism has to be pinpointed and dealt with before the animal is finally assigned.

So, one day the memorable event in the life of a young police dog comes to pass. He meets his new family. And vice versa. There is one important consideration: the family knows what to expect. The dog doesn't. The sudden change of locale, the exposure to a new group of strangers, is a trying experience for a sensitive animal. And many an apprehensive human can't help noting that the new member of the household could bite through small arms and legs. Therefore it can be well appreciated that some persons are not very much at ease during their first encounter with the "beast." This tension is immediately absorbed by the dog and emphasizes his own nervousness.

But, so far, there has not been a single instance when a dog hurt a member of his new family during the difficult days of getting acquainted. There may be frightening growls, but there are no bites.

Practically every day a police dog is being introduced to his human family somewhere in the United States. Interestingly enough, the dog's attitude and pace of development follows a very similar pattern.

A typical case which shows the reactions of the police

dog to his new family is that of Hobo, a two-year-old male German shepherd, black with white markings on his face, tipping the scales at eighty-five pounds. The dog went to live with his handler, officer Frank Best, twice Hobo's weight, twenty-nine years of age, who had spent five years on the police force. Frank's wife, Jean, was not much heavier than Hobo, and their only child, Barbara, four years old, was about half Hobo's weight. They lived in a residential district of a community not far from Los Angeles, California.

"Good Lord! That's a monster," flashed through Jean's mind and her arms reached out instinctively for her little daughter. Jean's gaze took in the head of a giant German shepherd framed in the window of a police car which had stopped in front of her house.

"Is he going to eat me?" asked the little girl, reflecting her mother's thoughts in a more concrete fashion. Barbara had been standing in front of the house for almost an hour, waiting.

Officer Frank Best stepped out of his car and approached his wife. He pointed to the dog. "The new member of our family." Then he went back to make sure that the car door was properly shut.

". . . But—but he's so huge," said Mrs. Best aloud. "I had no idea . . ."

Frank Best, still in uniform, walked back to his wife and little girl. He kissed Jean on the cheek and took Barbara in his arms.

"If he were a miniature dachshund he wouldn't do me any good as a partner. He is supposed to protect me."

Mrs. Best's eyes were still riveted on the animal caged in the car. The dog seemed to look at her threateningly.

"What's his name?" asked Barbara.

"I told you," answered her father, "his name is Hobo."

"Is he going to bite?" continued the little girl.

"Not the people he knows and likes," answered Frank.

"We're going to be his family and he isn't going to hurt anybody in his family."

At this moment the neighborhood tomcat passed by the Best house, right in front of Hobo. This brought forth a furious bark and Jean Best noticed to her horror a formidable array of white teeth, culminating in two dagger-like fangs.

"Quiet!" said Frank easily, and the barking stopped. The tomcat continued on his way, pretending nothing had happened.

"We might as well get acquainted," said Frank to his wife and daughter. "I'll be taking Hobo to his kennel. You just stay where you are and greet him quietly."

"The point is," said Jean regaining her composure and sense of humor, "will he greet *us* quietly?"

"He'll do what he is told," answered Frank. "He is very obedient and that's more than we can say of some people I know . . ." with a glance at Barbara.

The officer opened the door of the car, caressing the dog's head and at the same time preventing him from bursting out of the vehicle. He put the choker chain around the dog's neck and talked to him soothingly during the process. He knew it was not important *what* he said but *how* he said it.

"Okay, boy, we're going to show you your new house. Things will be a little strange for awhile, but before you know it you will realize that this is your new home. Jean and Barbara will become your family . . ."

Hobo looked at his master with intelligent, shiny eyes. But Frank could tell the dog was ill at ease.

Hobo, now on the leash, slid out of his car, his belly almost touching the ground. The dog looked at Jean and little Barbara with a mixture of curiosity and suspicion —the emphasis on the latter. Frank recognized the tenseness of the animal; the dog's hackles rose, revealing his excitement.

Frank continued to stroke the dog's head to calm him

down. "Now watch, Hobo," he said with a soothing voice, "you're going to meet two persons who will become very important in your life." The officer pointed to his wife and to his little girl. "This is Jean and this is Barbara."

"Hi, Hobo!" responded Barbara, loudly and clearly, completely oblivious of her recent thoughts concerning the dog. The girl made a quick step toward Hobo, prompting three instantaneous reactions:

Hobo growled. Jean yelled. Frank yanked on the choker chain.

"Sit!" ordered the officer quietly. The dog obeyed in a split second.

Frank looked at the little girl admonishingly. Barbara realized her mistake.

"I told you not to make any unexpected move," said Frank, "Hobo doesn't know who you are."

"He almost bit me," added Barbara in full agreement. "I'm sorry, Daddy. Sorry, Hobo."

"Don't forget to be careful," continued Frank. "Go ahead, Barbara, talk to Hobo. Talk to him very quietly."

"Okay, Daddy," said Barbara. Then she addressed the dog who watched that little human speculatively, his head tilted somewhat to one side.

"Hi, Hobo. I hope you will like me and my mommy. I think I'll like you; I certainly will if you never bite me . . ."

Frank turned to his wife, encouraging her to add a few chosen words to the event. Mrs. Best proved herself equal to the occasion.

"Welcome home, Hobo," she said. "You may be glad to know that you've just scared the living daylights out of me . . ."

"That was not his fault . . ." stated Frank. "I told the two of you what to do and what not to do when I arrived with him."

"Now be sure to stand still. Just relax . . ." Frank continued. "Hobo and I will be passing by and he may want to get a good sniff."

Hobo made the woman's acquaintance in his canine-like fashion.

"My turn?" asked Barbara eagerly, supressing the desire to execute a few tiny jumps.

"Not today," stated her mother.

"Please, Mommy, let Hobo sniff me . . ." exclaimed the little girl eagerly, as if this act would be the greatest honor anybody could bestow on her in the whole world.

Mrs. Best looked questioningly at her husband and saw him taking a firm grip on the leash.

"Well, certainly," said the man. "We don't show any preferences here. But remember. No unexpected moves."

Hobo greeted the child, who tried to make up her mind whether or not to be afraid.

"All right, everybody," said Frank. "That's enough introducing for today. I'm going to show Hobo his private quarters."

The officer and the dog walked along the driveway to the garage. Then Frank made a turn and opened a gate to the backyard. A new fence-enclosed kennel had been prepared with all the modern facilities. It had cost the city almost a thousand dollars to erect the cement structure. Frank opened the kennel door and released the dog. Hobo entered his private domain for the first time and began an immediate, thorough investigation.

"I'd better stay with the dog for a while so he doesn't feel lonely," said Frank.

"May I stay, too?" asked Barbara. "He'll feel even less lonely."

Frank could not detect any flaws in the child's logic. "All right, but keep your hands away from the fence."

Turning to Hobo, Frank said, "Good dog," and Hobo looked at his master, wagging his tail.

"Good doggie . . ." added Barbara, imitating her father's soothing tone. Hobo looked at the girl, motionless.

"Why doesn't he wag his tail for me?" asked Barbara wonderingly.

"He will when he is ready." Frank did not have any doubt.

"What do you think of Hobo?" asked Officer Frank Best when he finally rejoined his wife Jean in the kitchen.

"All I can think of are big teeth and . . ." she left the sentence unfinished and gestured towards Barbara. The little girl was busy opening Hobo's first can of food in the Best household, a privilege she had requested.

"We just have to be careful for a week or so," countered Frank, "until the dog knows who's who."

The first night with Hobo was not an occasion for much sleep in the Best household. Barbara wanted to say "good night" to Hobo. Prompted by the little girl's promise to go to bed immediately afterwards, Frank took her out to the kennel. But Barbara made the promise three times, inventing excuses for the repeat performance that would fluster a sage judge.

Then, as soon as Frank and Jean retired Hobo began to howl. And when Hobo howled he did so without reservations. Frank got up and had a number of talks with the dog, explaining that this was a neighborhood of working people who needed their sleep.

"Hobo understands," Frank said when he returned to his wife. "Somebody had to tell him!"

And the dog kept quiet for awhile.

"See," said Frank to his wife. "You just have to tell him. He isn't a mind reader."

Then the tomcat sauntered by again, in order to get another look at the neighborhood's latest addition. Naturally, Hobo let go with a tentative barrage of barks. The tomcat dissolved into the darkness.

A German shepherd and his handler meet another "dog with a badge" (STANLEY A. CHYNOWETH)

A German shepherd in training school hits the officer's sleeve in one jump while clearing the fence (STANLEY A. CHYNOWETH)

As part of this dog's training, he must scale a fence approximately nine feet high (ROYAL CANADIAN MOUNTED POLICE)

A German shepherd tracks with his master. When a dog is on a warm trail, he is strong and determined (ROYAL CANADIAN MOUNTED POLICE)

A training officer accustoms his dog to gunfire with blanks (STAN-LEY A. CHYNOWETH)

This dog has been ordered to attack (ROYAL CANADIAN MOUNTED POLICE)

A dog handler searches a prisoner while his German shepherd stands guard (ROYAL CANADIAN MOUNTED POLICE)

After his day at work with the law, this German shepherd relaxes with his handler's child (STANLEY A. CHYNOWETH)

"I'll bet something happened out there," said Officer Best to his wife. Both realized that they had been lying awake just to find out whether or not Hobo would behave. "Isn't it good to have a watchdog around the house?"

"Splendid," said Jean and, at last, permitted herself to relax. "I'm certainly glad he didn't wake up Barbara for another round of 'good-nights.'"

Hobo's second day started early. Barbara was up first; she had not been involved in the nocturnal problems of her parents. The first thing she intended to do was to go and see "him." As it became evident to her parents, references to "him" or sentences involving anything "he" did, pertained to Hobo. But there was only time for a brief visit to the kennel. Then Frank and Hobo had to take off for man's business, police work.

From then on Jean Best's day returned to its quiet routine—except for Barbara's constant figuring out the hours and minutes to be lived through until Hobo's return.

Frank and his dog arrived home a few minutes after four. According to a predetermined plan, Frank showed the dog first to his kennel. This was now a familiar place to the animal. After half an hour, another chapter in Hobo's life was about to begin. The dog was to be taken inside the house.

Jean and Barbara took their stations in the living room. Frank wanted them to be there before the dog entered. Then he went to the kennel, put Hobo on the leash, and prepared for his entrance. The dog, with Frank trailing after him, was encouraged to take a complete survey of the premises. Hobo looked over every nook and cranny, his big nose taking it all in. Returning to the living room, the dog was let off the leash.

Hobo promptly retired to a corner of the room, the corner nearest to Frank. From there he surveyed the peaceful scene, alert for something drastic to happen.

Frank watched the dog with one eye and his child with the other. He hoped Barbara, for once, would obey orders and stay still for a while. She did.

Jean turned to her husband. "I feel a little silly sitting like this in my own house." She looked quickly at the dog, who had her under concentrated observation.

"Just go about your business quietly," said Frank.

Jean got up and walked toward the kitchen. Hobo got up, too.

"Stay!" said Frank and the dog assumed his previous position.

"Come here, Barbara, sit next to me," continued Frank. The girl moved gladly over to her father.

"Isn't he going to bite anybody at all?" the child wanted to know.

"No, nobody in this house," explained her father.

"Also not if I touch him?" she continued, expressing an obvious desire.

"Don't touch him until he comes on his own and acts very friendly," said Frank.

"But how do I know he feels friendly?" Barbara wanted to know.

Frank took a long look at Hobo, then turned to his little daughter. "Somehow you can tell with animals. They let you know whether they like you or whether they are going to attack you."

Frank turned on the television set. Hobo pricked his ears. For a minute or so he looked at the tube suspiciously. Then he turned to Frank to see whether he showed any unusual reaction to the moving pattern on the screen. Since his master was completely relaxed, Hobo decided that no dangerous forces were at work.

It was a peaceful scene at the Best house. Frank looked at the television. Barbara looked at Hobo. Hobo looked at Frank. As Jean dared to cross the room between Hobo and Frank an ever so slight trace of a growl emanated from Hobo's corner. A brief, stern look from Frank quieted him.

After an hour or so Frank took Hobo back to his kennel where the dog stayed for the entire night. Everybody slept well.

On the third day, Hobo was permitted to stay in the house a little longer. But the dog remained as reserved as ever. The only person he liked was his master. The dog eyed Jean with unconcealed suspicion and looked through Barbara as if she did not exist.

"What good is it to have a dog," said the girl, "when you cannot touch him and if he does not play with you. My toy dogs are better."

All the same, Jean became a little more relaxed and Frank believed that the most critical period was over. But this relaxation did not seem to register on the dog. He always assumed his position in the same living room corner, his eyes watching his master.

By the fifth day of police dog Hobo's presence in the Best household, the animal still did not show any change in attitude toward the officer's wife and child. He simply stayed out of their way, assuming a polite aloofness. There were no more growls, but Jean began to wonder whether the dog would ever change; whether the stranger in the house would ever become a part of the family.

During that afternoon, Jean was busy ironing in the kitchen. Frank was in the living room, repairing a lamp. Barbara played on the living room floor with a couple of toy dogs, an obvious substitution for the real dog, who was lying in his corner, seemingly sulking, his half-closed eyes trained in the direction of his master.

After a while, Barbara got up from the floor and walked into her own bedroom, which was right next to the living room. As the little girl made her inconspicuous exit, Hobo's head went up and the dog's ears formed two high triangles. Then, slowly, he rose and followed Barbara into her room. Neither Frank nor Jean noticed that the child and the dog were by themselves, a situation that was supposed to be avoided at all costs.

As long as they live Frank and his wife Jean will never forget any of the next split seconds.

The first thing they heard was Hobo's ferocious growl from the direction of Barbara's room.

An instant later there was the sound of splintering furniture. Then—the bloodchilling scream of the tomcat which, as Jean pointed out later, sounded like a small child.

Frank reached the door of Barbara's room in two big steps. The lamp in his hands went crashing to the floor. Jean, feeling faint, rushed behind him.

But the scene in front of them did not permit any thoughts of danger.

Barbara was not hurt at all. The little girl turned to her parents and giggled. Then she declared beamingly:

"He kissed me! He kissed me!"

At this moment Hobo returned from the outside, making his way easily through the remnants of a smashed screen door. As if to demonstrate visually what the girl tried to convey to her parents, the dog turned his giant head to Barbara. He gave her face a quick lick from chin to forehead. There never was a happier girl.

It was not overly difficult for Policeman Frank Best to realize what had happened. His daughter provided most of the information.

Barbara had gone to her room to look for another stuffed dog among her toys, her way of compensating for Hobo's antisocial behavior. Suddenly she found herself face to face with the big German shepherd, who had followed her without making a sound. The dog looked at the little girl seriously and the child realized instinctively that there was nothing to be afraid of. She forgot all the rules her father had so patiently explained to her about the dog, and had put her arms around Hobo's neck and kissed him right on the nose. Somebody had to break this stalemate between her and the dog. Who wanted to cuddle a toy dog when someone wonderful like Hobo was around?

Hobo considered the child's action for a brief moment and then reciprocated in kind. At this very moment the curious tomcat came along and glanced through the screen door. Hobo, not in the mood to put up with any outsider at this solemn moment, hurled himself at the cat, ignoring the screen door. The tomcat, exploding a bloodcurdling scream, had practically rocketed up a tree in front of the house.

"I want Hobo to kiss me again," said Barbara, full of enthusiasm.

The man of the house decided to take advantage of this emotional momentum generated by the dog and child. He turned to Jean: "Come on. You call Hobo now and make friends with him as well."

Jean turned to the dog. "Come here, Hobo, we've got to get acquainted. Orders from Headquarters."

Hobo approached the woman slowly, his tail at medium wag. He permitted Jean to pat his head and to be scratched behind the ears. For a few seconds the woman and the dog eyed each other apprehensively. Then they decided to become friends. It was all over their faces, and to avoid any trace of doubt Hobo's tail shifted into high.

As far as the dog was concerned, the Best family was officially adopted. It was "his" family against the entire world. Therefore, intruders had better beware.

Hobo's integration into the social life of the community was the next stage to be accomplished. All the relatives and acquaintances of the Best family had to be alerted not to arrive unexpectedly, and to avoid an impressive entrance at all costs. The neighbors were introduced to the dog systematically. A big sign was posted in front of the house stating that this was the domain of a dangerous dog and, anyhow, the person coming close enough to read the sign was receiving matching sound effects while Hobo was at home.

A visitor who was to meet Hobo for the first time had to undergo a definite ceremonial. He had to be properly introduced to the dog by Jean or Frank. Then a gesture of friendship had to be performed for the benefit of Hobo. Only then did the dog relax.

Hobo's attitude toward persons visiting the Best household showed a definite pattern. It soon developed that Hobo was a class-conscious canine. Any social equal of the family was treated by the dog with patient tolerance —the highest degree of emotion Hobo was able to muster for an outsider. Friends, relatives, and neighbors were left pretty much alone after passing the initial inspection.

But salesmen, delivery boys, repairmen, and, naturally, the universal canine target—the mailman—had to put up with the dog's unconcealed hostility. They were continuously under surveillance and were greeted with terrible snarls, retracted lips, and ferocious looks. But nobody was ever touched by the dog during such shows of strength. Frank, who knew the dog thoroughly, was sure that Hobo was actually having fun during such demonstrations.

Barbara's friends, the children of the neighborhood, got along with Hobo famously. Having his ears, tail, or legs pulled did not bother the animal. If too many children were pestering him, Hobo just shook them off and stayed out of reach. But during the greatest turmoil and confusion, Hobo's eyes were always trained in Barbara's direction.

Hobo's tremendous protective instinct never let him completely relax when a visitor was in the house. It took Frank a while to recognize all the signs of this attitude. Hobo had the habit of placing himself between the visitor and his master. This was not done in an ostentatious way; if the visitor or Frank changed position, Hobo would get up, stretch, and then lie down somewhere between the two. If more than one person were present, Hobo could be found in front of Frank, his half-closed eyes looking over the guests.

A few weeks after Hobo was first brought to the Best home, Frank was resting in his yard, reading the evening paper. As he looked up, he saw little Barbara and two of her friends cavorting with the big German shepherd. The dog was acting like a playful puppy, which made the children squeal with delight.

Only a few hours ago Frank had flushed out half a dozen suspects from a warehouse. He had placed the six men against a wall and ordered Hobo to guard them while he went back to his squad car to call in for assistance. When he came back the men stood exactly where he had left them, their hands up and their eyes converging on the dog, who performed his repertoire of threats whenever one of the men even dared to move a finger. Hobo was indeed a horrible "monster" from the suspects' point of view.

Then Frank remembered that he himself did not present the picture of a kind father and husband at that time. He was a determined, hard cop who would not have hesitated to use all the force at his command if necessary. As the master was, so was the dog.

6

The Victim

Rinnie, a German shepherd, was the pride and joy of the Wichita, Kansas, Police Department. As the top dog of an excellent canine unit, he had an impressive number of arrests to his credit.

Rinnie and his handler, John Judge, had frequently been honored for outstanding police achievements, and the dog was the receiver of the Lassie Gold Medal, one of the highest awards given for canine accomplishments. Frequent TV appearances and newspaper stories of the dog-man team enhanced the popularity of the animal, and aided in the promotion of good relations between civilians and police officers.

Many localities introducing police dogs in their programs encounter considerable resistance. The reasons are fear that the dog may attack law-abiding citizens, hate for animals in general and dogs in particular, and ignorance

of a dog's part within a law enforcement machinery.
There are also members in police departments with the
sincere belief that dogs do not justify the investment in
time and money necessary for initiation and maintenance of a canine unit.

Obviously, the anti-dog faction exults whenever a
member of a police dog unit is found guilty of a blunder.
In the same way, attacks against the police in general are
launched if one man in a force of thousands is derelict in
his duties.

It was no other than police dog Rinnie who gave the
dog-haters of Wichita ample ammunition for their cause.
It was December, 1960, and Rinnie was at the peak of his
career, a highly respected member of the Wichita Police
Department. Yet at that time it seemed that this dog had
committed the worst blunder possible.

On December 27, the complaint board at the Wichita
Police Headquarters was lit up like a Christmas tree. The
officer who operated the board received and processed the
unusual array of calls. Many of them had their special
Christmas connotation: an office party getting out of
hand; accidents caused by drunk drivers; pickpockets attempting to get their share of Yule; and suicide attempts,
which are especially prevalent during the holidays.

The men on the Force were well familiar with seasonal
demand for their services. The entire department was on
duty or standing by. So was the canine unit, just in case
a situation might develop demanding the special talents
of the dogs.

Some of the men were clustered around a makeshift
Christmas tree in the slightly overheated squad room,
hoping not to be called out into the cold winter night. But
the men knew that this was a vain hope, indeed.

Another red light blinked on the board. The receiving
police officer pressed a switch to take the incoming call.

"Wichita Police Department," he said in his impersonal manner.

A strained voice came from the other end of the line.

"Talk a little slower," said the officer. At the same time he pressed a button that sounded a buzzer in the Detective Division. A white light blinking on the board indicated that one of the investigators was listening in.

"Was just held up," said the voice on the other end of the line. "Kidnapped in my own car. Two money bags were taken away from me . . ."

"What is your name, sir?" The officer's voice was firm and friendly. He wanted the caller to compose himself.

"Chuck Smith . . ."

"And where are you calling from?"

"The Quality Liquor Store on St. Francis Avenue . . . It's the first telephone I could reach . . ."

"All right, Mr. Smith, just stay where you are. One of the squad cars will be there in a couple of minutes."

The watch commander dispatched a number of cars cruising in the field to the address given by Smith. Inasmuch as tracking might be a possibility, he ordered Patrolman John Judge and his dog Rinnie to join the investigating team.

As the officers reached Chuck Smith at the liquor store, the holdup victim had regained some of his composure. He reported in greater detail what had happened to him just a short while ago. He was an employee of a market chain; one of his duties was to collect the receipts every night from a number of branch stores. The money was taken to the main office, counted, and then deposited in a special night drop in one of Wichita's major banks.

That evening, after picking up two money bags containing about two thousand dollars in checks and cash, Smith said, he brought his car to a halt at an intersection and waited for the traffic to clear in order to cross over.

Suddenly a heavyset man appeared out of nowhere, opened the door of Smith's car and forced his way in.

"Drive on!" ordered the man. "Do what I say if you know what's good for you." To emphasize this, he threatened Smith with a blue steel revolver in a gloved hand. Smith did not feel this was the time to put up an argument and continued to drive.

"Go to the north end of the town and don't waste any time," the gunman demanded. Smith complied. He was looking for a police car and planned to commit a traffic violation, hoping to attract the officer's attention. But no police car came in sight during the entire forced trip along the streets of Wichita.

The gunman, who seemed to know exactly what he was after, rummaged in the back of Smith's car. He located the money bags and shifted them to the front seat. Then he noted a five-pound canned ham which Smith had received from his employers as a Christmas gift. He added this to the pile.

After awhile, the bandit told Smith, "Pull over here. I'm getting out."

His gun always trained on Smith, the man waited for the car to stop. He took the two money bags and ran north, disappearing in the dark December night. Smith then drove on, and looked for a telephone to call the police. "He took my ham along as well," concluded the victim with an injured expression.

The officers decided on their first move, and drove to the intersection where the bandit had left Smith's car. Inasmuch as the suspect wore gloves, as Smith had remembered, it was of little value to leave the car behind and have the crime lab check for fingerprints. Smith's car would be put to better use. Police dog Rinnie might be able to pick up the gunman's scent and could attempt tracking. Smith could point out the direction where the crook had taken off.

Arriving at the holdup scene, Smith gave another exact account of what had happened. He pointed out where he had stopped the car where the suspect had disappeared. The men went over the area carefully.

At this point of the investigation, Patrolman John Judge and police dog Rinnie joined the other police personnel. The dog's master was familiarized with the situation.

Rinnie was led to Smith's car and ordered to jump up on the right front seat to pick up the scent of the robber. Chuck Smith, who was standing on the left side of the car, observed the dog's action with interest. After a minute or so, Rinnie stopped sniffing and looked at her master. The dog's behavior told Judge that the animal knew all he had to.

"All right, Rinnie, come down," said the dog handler easily.

Rinnie jumped out of the car. Without hesitation, but also without undue haste, the dog ran around the car to Smith, who was talking to one of the detectives, his back towards the approaching dog. Before his handler could utter a command, the dog bit Smith in the seat of his pants.

Rinnie's handler was flabbergasted. It seemed obvious what must have happened. The dog had picked up the wrong scent, the scent of the car owner—the victim of the holdup. The most inexperienced police dog would not make such a clumsy mistake, let alone the celebrated Rinnie.

John Judge reprimanded his dog severely. Strangely enough, the animal did not show the signs of embarrassment or remorse that he usually did when talked to sharply, even for a very minor fault. On the contrary, the dog wagged his expressive tail and looked up at his master as if to say, "Didn't I do a good job?" Rinnie's actions were confusing to say the least.

While Chuck Smith was taken to a nearby hospital for first aid, John Judge and Rinnie were sent back to Headquarters. The news about Rinnie's mistake spread like wildfire and was featured by all the news media. It is still news when a dog bites a man.

Rinnie's misdeed was a welcome event for the anti-dog faction. Letters were dispatched to the chief and the mayor. A thorough investigation of the incident was requested and Rinnie was suspended from the Force. The Canine Corps was in jeopardy.

But Rinnie's friends did not stay idle either. After the first shock subsided, John Judge discussed the case with the chief trainer. They felt that the dog was above making such an elementary mistake and were beginning to investigate other than the obvious conclusion—that the dog had followed the wrong scent.

The Detective Division continued working on the case, dog bite or not, as there was an unsolved holdup on their hands. Under the supervision of the police chief, several detectives proceeded with the investigation.

One of the detectives began delving into Chuck Smith's story and background. He discovered that pieces of Smith's story did not quite fit together. The more the detective searched, the more weak links came to the surface.

After several days of checking and rechecking, the detective asked Smith to come to Police Headquarters. He persuaded the man to submit to a lie detector test. Smith said he had nothing to hide.

As Smith talked, the vacillating pens inscribed their strange patterns on the moving paper tape of the polygraph recorder. Two police officers watched with considerable curiosity, for the machine indicated that the detective's gamble paid off. Chuck Smith was lying.

With this additional knowledge, and other information collected about Smith, it was not difficult for the detective to break the man down during further interrogation. He obtained a confession which solved the holdup and, what was more important to some of the people of the Force, vindicated police dog Rinnie.

Smith said his job collecting money was too tempting to resist. He and his accomplice, Phil Thompson, had been planning for some time to steal the money. They decided to fake a robbery and to split the loot.

On the night of the fake holdup, Smith phoned his accomplice to tell him that the collections would be substantial. The two met at a street corner. Thompson took the money bags from Smith's car, hailed a taxi and drove home. Smith called the police, playing the "victim."

The detectives did not lose any time. They loaded Smith into a squad car and drove to Phil Thompson's apartment. The suspect was not at home. After a quick search the officers found most of the money, including about five hundred dollars in cash, hidden at the bottom of a dresser drawer in the man's bedroom.

Smith, the self-made "holdup victim," was one of the very few people in Wichita who was not proud of police dog Rinnie, who was immediately reinstated.

"What can you do," mumbled Smith, "when you're up against a dog that can read your mind and then against some machine that knows whether or not you're telling the truth?"

"But," as handler John Judge was to tell everyone for weeks to come, " . . . it took Rinnie just one quick sniff to get at the truth. The polygraph machine needed much more time."

A big question, thoroughly discussed in the squad room, and then by dog trainers all over the country, was: "How did Rinnie know?"

Was it a coincidence? Impossible. Rinnie hadn't ever bitten anybody before. Was it instinct? Perhaps. Animals have a sixth sense, and can tell right from wrong in many cases.

The most accepted theory is that Rinnie could "smell" Smith's uneasiness, resulting from his lie to the officers. To dogs, people may have a smell of guilt.

A dog and a polygraph; both are used by a modern police department, both proving their place in progressive criminology, and both are in the hands of specialists in their new fields.

7

The Case
of the Empty Carton

Flying eastbound out of Los Angeles at night, an airplane pilot has no difficulty in spotting Las Vegas. For, after dusk, this city tries to outdo the midday sun. The blaze of millions of multicolored lights of downtown Las Vegas carves an oasis of brilliance out of the desert. Enormous signs invite the tourist to go to such well-known establishments as "The Last Frontier," "The Golden Nugget," "The Green Mint," and the "Fremont." Fourteen million people a year follow the lure of this Nevada town.

Once inside one of those gambling palaces the visitors, well endowed with a will to lose, find themselves confronted with battalions of one-armed bandits. These mechanical collectors and their human operators are more than willing to accommodate all comers and hold them up for their nickels, dimes, and quarters.

But one-armed bandits are not the only species of holdup-men in this town, which is located in the state with the highest crime rate in the USA. Las Vegas has its proportionate share of the two-armed variety, and their victims are less cooperative than the visitors of the slot machine and other gambling establishments. Least cooperative of all are the members of the Las Vegas Police Department, who deal as a matter of daily routine with this two-armed species. And on numerous occasions the officers are aided in their actions by four-legged assistants—the police dogs.

The Canine Corps of the Las Vegas Police Department started its operation early in 1962, when eight German shepherds joined the force. Every dog was assigned to one officer who had to take a course in police dog procedure, first by himself and then with his future four-legged companion. The man-dog teams chalked up such a consistent record of achievement that, today, the department would not think to do without them.

The following Las Vegas police case shows the type of situation in which a dog excels and, because of his sense of smell, can do the work of a squad of men. This outstanding canine demonstration became known as "The Case of the Empty Carton."

Officers Fuller and Holloway had been on their graveyard shift for half an hour. Their squad car made its way through downtown Las Vegas. The two men kept their eyes on the throngs of humanity who went about their way in a fashion reminiscent of Times Square at noon.

People react to this town according to their temperaments and objectives. The majority want to gamble away their money in a setup with the odds admittedly against them. Some sacrifice a few hard-earned dollars; the big-time spender is ready to throw away a fortune for kicks; the habitués of the town are on their way to their favorite gambling palace, looking neither left nor right; and there are, as well, the army of employees who keep the place humming twenty-four hours a day, every day in the year.

Fuller stopped the police car at a pedestrian crossing. Suddenly both men reacted to a sound and looked at each other for confirmation. Through the din of the traffic they made out the ringing of a burglar alarm. Fuller stepped on the gas and turned the vehicle in the direction of the alarm. The officers listened to the radio for any indication of a burglary report.

As the squad car rounded a corner, the sound of the alarm increased, and the men approached the Thrifty Drugstore. The alarm system of this store had gone off. Fuller stopped the car and his partner stepped out to check the front of the drugstore for evidence of forceful entry. At the same time, Fuller made a call to headquarters to report the incident. Then he drove on to enter the alley behind the drugstore and check the delivery entrance located there. The officers did not find any suspicious signs either in the front or in the rear of the premises. So far it was all routine procedure.

The lieutenant at Police Headquarters to whom Fuller's call was immediately reported put certain elements of his command in motion. First, he ordered two additional mobile units to the Thrifty Drugstore. Then a call went to the Burglar Alarm Company. As he had assumed, one of the guards was already on his way, for these people kept their radios tuned in on the police wave length. At last, the lieutenant telephoned Officer Johnston of the canine unit, ordering him and his German shepherd, Burgie, to proceed to the drugstore as well.

Within a few minutes after reporting the alarm, Fuller and Holloway were joined by four other police officers and the guard from the Burglar Alarm Company. This man had a key to the building. He opened the door and they entered, their guns ready. Fuller, in the squad car, was still stationed at the rear of the drugstore.

The police officers did not see any signs of disturbance but they started a systematic search of the three-story building. Every room, every possible hiding place was checked. All sliding doors of the counters were opened to look for a suspect. But the searchers did not find anyone.

"Looks like another false alarm to me," said Holloway.

False burglar alarms, more frequent than false fire alarms, are indeed a problem for the police all over the country, adding to the workload of the personnel. It is estimated that about 90 per cent of the alarms are set off accidentally, for most of the devices are activated by vibrations. These can be produced by the passing of a heavy truck, sonic booms of an airplane, by cats, mice, or rats. And naturally, in the case of a slight earthquake, every self-respecting vibration alarm goes off. Newer devices, operating electronically, are a great improvement, and often they are silent alarms hooked up to a central control station.

The search was almost completed when the canine unit arrived.

The man from the Alarm Company looked at Burgie with little enthusiasm. He did not care for canine competition.

"Just combed the place. It's clean," he said to Officer Johnston. The dog handler looked at the sergeant in charge, who knew that this was only the second time Burgie had been used on a case.

"Might as well give the dog a run for our money, now that he's here," the sergeant said. "Go ahead, you two, but don't make a production of it."

"Okay, Sergeant," said Johnston, and let the dog off the leash. The handler studied Burgie's reactions with great care, realizing that the animal was confronted with a difficult task. A multitude of people had walked through the aisles of the large drugstore all day long, served by dozens of employees. After closing, the maintenance people cleaned the entire place, stocked the counters, and got everything ready for the next day. There was a whole panorama of smells for Burgie.

On the other hand, if a burglar had entered the store after everyone had left, there could be a hot track for the dog. But Johnston knew that many such burglars entered the premises during business hours, concealed themselves, and emerged when the place was vacated. Some burglars spent the night and left the store the next day, among the cash-paying customers. This procedure, incidentally, became very fashionable in New York and other large city department stores a few years ago. Some of them began employing watch dogs on a permanent basis. The animals were let loose at night to flush out the uninvited guests. The mere presence of the dogs put an end to this lucrative type of shoplifting.

Johnston and Burgie started their routine search on the top floor. There were no results. The dog was alert, but his attention did not seem to focus on any one area. Gradually they made their way to the main floor.

There, the dog ran all over the place, becoming somewhat more agitated. Although he sniffed and barked, he still did not connect with any definite track. Whenever Johnston called the dog, Burgie ran to his master, but indicated that he did not want to give up the search.

"Waste of your time and mine," said the man from the Alarm Company. "Let's get out of here so I can lock the joint."

Burgie, in the meantime, crossed and recrossed the main floor of the drugstore, running through the aisles with increasing agitation, but still in an undecided manner. Finally, he approached a door leading to the basement. He stood there for a few seconds, sniffing the

floor in front of it. Johnston suddenly felt the dog was
making up his mind. Then Burgie looked back at his
master and barked excitedly.

"I think Burgie wants to have a look at the basement,"
Johnston said to the sergeant.

The Alarm Company man remained quiet, but his expression revealed his impatience with the dog routine.
The sergeant, however, felt the dog should have his will.
"I'll be on until eight in the morning," he said. "Let's give
the basement another quick once-over. Then we can wrap
it up."

Johnston opened the door to the basement, while another officer turned on the light. Burgie dove downstairs
with a few long leaps and immediately started an excited
search.

The basement served mainly as a storeroom. Merchandise was piled up all over the place and some of the
articles were still in their original shipping containers.
The officers had already searched the area carefully, and
had found nothing.

Some of the cardboard cartons were of considerable
size; they were used for bulky but very light articles such
as paper napkins and other paper articles.

Burgie, closely followed by Johnston, did not waste any
more time. He ran through one of the aisles of stacked
merchandise and, with a sudden singleness of purpose,
attacked one of the large cardboard cartons. The reaction
of the carton was immediate.

Surprisingly, the assaulted box came to life. The
two top lids swung open and a man's body appeared,
his hands reaching for the ceiling.

Burgie's reaction to the apparition was a veritable barrage of barks, growls, and a show of his white teeth for
good measure. The commotion attracted the officers who
had waited on the main floor. They came running down
the stairway, their weapons ready to shoot.

The burglar completely disregarded the police officers

converging upon him. He just stared at Burgie. Johnston ordered Burgie to "guard," and the dog froze, his eyes on the suspect and a deep growl still emanating from his throat.

The man finally found his voice. "Keep this vicious hound off me will you?" he begged. "I'm unarmed, don't you see?"

Johnston stepped forward and turned to the suspect.

"He won't hurt you as long as you don't try any funny business. Come on!"

The burglar climbed out of the carton. Some of the men could not help but smile, but it was no funny business to the burglar. His eyes never wandered from the dog.

The sergeant had recognized the suspect immediately, for he was a repeater and on the "wanted" list.

It was not difficult to reconstruct this case. The suspect had entered the store a few minutes before closing time, found a hiding place in one of the utility rooms, and stayed there until all the personnel were gone. He allowed himself a couple of hours' rest in one of the folding chairs, figuring he would make an easier getaway after midnight.

Collecting a good haul of narcotic-type drugs and pep pills from the prescription counter, the burglar put them in several big shopping bags and started to leave the establishment. But in the process of opening the door, he set off the burglar alarm. He could not leave the store quickly enough because a group of men were standing near the exit. Then, before he knew it, the first police car was on the scene. He rushed into the basement and hid in one of the empty cartons, for he had successfully avoided arrest in this fashion once before. The suspect thought he had made it again, until Burgie smelled him out.

The officers searching the basement had not realized

that some of the large shipping cartons were empty. But this complicated setup for human police officers was an ideal situation for Burgie.

The Thrifty Drugstore burglar started a long stretch at the Nevada State Penitentiary.

8

The Specialist

The German shepherd is universally accepted for police work on account of his great range of physical and mental skills. Every now and then, one of these dogs may develop an unusual talent in addition to his overall knowledge of police work. Captain, an amazing German shepherd in one capital city of the United States, is the four-footed nemesis of narcotics peddlers. Where the human eye is useless, the uncanny ability of Captain to sniff out the drugs has resulted in a number of arrests of suspected peddlers and users. Captain works with his handler, Frank Lewis, and the two have become an important element of the Narcotics Detail of their police department. Here is an example of the dog's investigative powers, in a case which confounded the police detectives.

August, 1962, was hot and humid, and the heat had its effect on a man who was walking down the city streets.

The night lights showed his shadowy growth of beard and messy hair that had not been touched by a barber's scissors for weeks. The man wore a sweatshirt, levis, and a pair of sneakers without socks. He crossed the street and approached a small hamburger place.

A flickering neon sign revealed the name of the establishment, "Joe's Burgers." But the proprietor's name was not Joe. It was Mike Pollard, alias Ted Kennard, alias Terrence Anders—or so the files of the Narcotics Detail indicated.

The man entered "Joe's." Mike, a man in his late fifties, was behind the counter, attempting to tune an old radio. There was only one other customer, slouched over a racing form.

"One hamburger—medium," said the newcomer to Mike, "on a Kaiser roll." And then he added in a conspiratorial tone: "It's for Danny . . ."

Mike studied the man on the other side of the counter, from his uncombed hair to his sweaty sneakers. Then, without as much as saying a word, he took a hamburger patty from the big, rusty refrigerator and threw it on the hot stove.

"Cut out the funny business," the man whispered to Mike. "You know what I came for."

Mike took a Kaiser roll from a glass container and cut it in half with a long, sharp knife.

"Funny business?"

"You know I don't want a burger," said the man in a low voice, with a furtive glance at the other customer.

"I don't know what the devil you're talking about," said Mike, turning over the meat patty and watching an oversupply of fat spreading across the hot plate.

"Danny said you'll fix me up," said the man, his nervous fingers drumming the counter.

"I'm aimin' to," answered Mike, pointing to the stove, "the best hamburgers this part of the country."

The man pulled a ten-dollar bill from his pants pocket and showed it to Mike. "I'll need some grass. I'll be a steady customer."

"Burgers and franks, that's all you get here. And no salad," answered Mike.

The man returned the ten-dollar bill to his pocket and turned to leave.

"That will be four bits," Mike said sharply, pointing at the sizzling hamburger. "I ain't going to eat it myself."

The man waited. Mike put the food in a paper bag and handed it to the man, who threw two quarters on the counter.

"You know you're not the only place in this city," he said and left. Mike rang up the sale on the cash register, a picture of the law-abiding citizen.

A nondescript Chevrolet was parked about half a block down the street from "Joe's." The car faced the hamburger place, and its two occupants showed considerable interest in the activities of the small restaurant. As the unkempt man left "Joe's," he walked towards the parked car. Passing the vehicle, he shook his head and, with a deft swing, pitched the bag through the window of the car and walked on.

The two men looked at each other disappointedly.

"Mike isn't the easiest guy to trip up," said the younger man to the other.

The older man answered, "He was tripped up before; he'll be tripped up again. It's part of the game."

The younger man opened the paper bag and produced the hamburger. He looked at his companion and asked, "Do you think it's any good? I'm hungry."

"Mike's very careful not to break any laws of the Health Department. Eat it. It's on our citizens."

As the younger man took a tentative bite, his partner started the car and drove off . . .

The next day, a meeting took place at the Narcotics Detail at Police Headquarters. Present was the man who had attempted to buy some marijuana from Mike. He turned out to be a detective borrowed from a nearby police department. His beard was gone, his hair was well combed and his freshly pressed summer suit made it difficult to see in him the addict who was at "Joe's." He talked with a lieutenant and a sergeant about their unsuccessful attempt the night before. The lieutenant was leading the conversation.

"We know that Mike's place is a retail outlet for marijuana. As a matter of fact, one of our informers bought some last night." He turned to the detective, "After you got your hamburger."

"Well, I tried."

"I know," answered the lieutenant. "Mike has his guard up. I think he sells the stuff only to customers he knows personally."

"And we've got to catch him in the act," added the sergeant.

The telephone rang on the lieutenant's desk. He answered it, and after a brief conversation turned to the others. "That was the Chief. I had a talk with him this morning and asked him for clearance to raid Mike's place. He just okayed it."

"I thought you wanted to avoid a raid."

"I don't like it," the lieutenant answered, "but we need some action." Then he explained to the detective: "It's far from sure that we will find any evidence, and even if we do Mike has the habit of playing the saint. Somebody else always has planted the grass. He is innocent." The lieutenant turned to the sergeant. "Try to get Captain and Lewis. They may save us lots of time."

Noticing the detective's inquisitive look, the sergeant explained that Captain was a police dog.

The raid took place the following morning. The lieutenant, the sergeant, and two officers entered "Joe's" prior to opening hour. Officer Lewis, with his especially equipped Canine Corps car, waited outside.

Mike didn't spread any welcome mat for the early visitors. After looking over the search warrant presented by the lieutenant, he resigned himself with the air of a real pro. He even offered some coffee to the men, a friendly gesture that did not strike a responsive chord.

"I assure you, you won't find a thing, Lieutenant. This place is clean and I'm going clean. Got a good little business here."

The officers searched the place in a calm, systematic manner. Mike shrugged his shoulders and then continued to get his place in shape for the expected breakfast customers.

The men went through all the shelves and all sorts of containers. They examined the refrigerator and looked for loose floorboards.

"I told you," said Mike proudly. "This place is clean. You guys already wasted twenty minutes."

The lieutenant looked at his watch. Then he walked outside and talked to Officer Lewis, who was standing in front of his car: "Come on, get Captain. Maybe he can come up with something."

Lewis opened the cage at the rear of the automobile and Captain jumped out, his tail wagging with eager anticipation.

"Come on, boy," said the handler to his dog, "let's show 'em what we can do!"

As the animal entered the place, Mike made some nasty remarks about sending vicious dogs after peaceful citizens. Lewis found those remarks very interesting. He knew from experience that only people with a bad conscience talk in this fashion, people who have something to hide. So he felt sure that Mike was guilty.

Captain, in the meantime, started his own type of investigation. His nose close to the ground, he was running back and forth through the hamburger place. Captain's colleagues left him a free field.

Mike watched the dog tensely.

Lewis, who had an intimate knowledge of the animal's reactions, recognized a tautness in Captain's behavior which showed when the dog smelled a trace of narcotics. But Captain continued to crisscross the area, without being able to pinpoint a specific location.

"All right, you've had your fun," said Mike to the officers. "Now, if you don't mind, let me open up for business. Some of my customers prefer their breakfast without the police, no offense meant, and without a dog sniffing at their feet."

At the same moment Captain stopped in front of the big refrigerator, sniffed, looked for a moment at Lewis and barked.

"Open it up!" the lieutenant ordered Mike.

"Stop the comedy," the suspect answered.

"Open that refrigerator," repeated the lieutenant.

"All right," said Mike. "But I don't want this dog sniffing around in my refrigerator. Health laws, you know. And I don't want to break any laws."

"Just open it," said the lieutenant firmly.

"Well," said Mike, "if you guys have all this time to waste, that's your business. But let's get this over with so I can take care of my business. I've got to make money to pay taxes."

The large refrigerator door was opened, revealing an ample supply of bottles, milk containers, hamburger patties, and cartons of frankfurters. Captain continued to bark and to sniff. Officer Lewis knew that they were on the right track. He signaled this to the lieutenant.

One of the lower shelves of the refrigerator contained a

big box filled with frankfurters in special packages made up by the supplier for restaurants. These frankfurters attracted Captain's attention.

"Look, you guys," Mike yelled, "if this lousy dog wants to eat, I'll give him some meat. But don't let him spoil my supply."

Captain barked more and more excitedly. Then he started digging through the ten pounds of frankfurters, pawing them apart.

When the dog reached the bottom of the large box, he found what he was looking for. There were twelve bricks of marijuana, well camouflaged by the frankfurter wrappings. The odor of the meat was supposed to confuse the animal, and the wrappings were to hide the marijuana from the men.

The police officers examined the evidence. Mike, as expected, presented a picture of amazement. He professed innocence and suggested that somebody must have entered the place at night and planted the stuff.

The lieutenant reminded Mike that he claimed the same thing the last time he was arrested on an identical charge.

"Sure," answered Mike. "I was innocent then. Just as I'm innocent now."

Mike did not open his place of business that morning. He was booked on suspicion of possessing marijuana and taken to headquarters for questioning. His attorney got him out on bail the same day.

The lieutenant congratulated Captain and Officer Lewis on their accomplishment. On the way to Headquarters, Lewis stopped at a delicatessen and bought a pound of frankfurters for the dog. This was the first time that Captain had had to bypass frankfurters in line of duty, and he liked sausages better than any other food.

But this case was far from over. Mike Pollard and his lawyer tried everything to absolve the man from this new charge. Mike even stated that the marijuana was planted by the police in order to obtain publicity for Captain.

Officer Lewis and Captain did not let those accusations interfere with their work. As a matter of fact, this summer month was one of the busiest times of their career. Captain's nose was responsible for making a big dent in the marijuana traffic in his city. His remarkable sense of smell sniffed out dope in all types of hiding places: in trouser cuffs and pockets; under car floorboards; in trash cans.

Captain's and Officer Lewis's continuous chain of successes was duly reported by the press, radio, and television. This news disproved Mike Pollard's accusation that the raid at "Joe's" was just a publicity stunt for the dog. After all, a good police dog produces his own, genuine news.

9

Above and Beyond the Call of Duty

It was three o'clock in the morning of March 17, 1961. Officer Vernon Scoville drove his squad car along the streets of Kansas City, Missouri. Arriving at an intersection, he turned into the parking lot of a fish market. Scoville stopped the car, opened the door, and stepped out.

The officer was not alone. With him was another member of the Kansas City Police Department, the police dog Trooper. The seventy-five pound German shepherd was relatively new at the job; he had been on active duty for only seven months.

Trooper jumped from the car, right on the heels of his handler. Both man and dog felt the night cold enveloping them. But neither had a premonition that they would be put to a supreme test in a very short time.

So far the graveyard shift had been routine. According to his orders, the officer was systematically checking certain areas. The fish market and its surroundings was just one of them. Vernon Scoville turned off the headlights of his patrol car. It was pitch dark and very quiet. The shops and stands were locked up for the night. But before dawn all that would change. The first sellers and buyers would appear and this would become a noisy, crowded place.

But now there was no sound. The stillness of the area was accentuated by the noise of a heavy truck rumbling down a distant street. Vernon Scoville felt the cold nose of the dog touching his left hand for a brief moment. "You're not alone," Trooper seemed to say in this fashion. "I'm with you."

Officer Scoville was grateful for the dog's companionship. It made the time go faster, made his duty easier, and gave him a feeling of security. Vernon Scoville scratched the dog between his ears. "Good boy, Trooper," he whispered. "I'm certainly glad you're with me." Trooper's tail wagged in response. If the dog had his way, he would not let his master out of his sight—ever.

Yet Trooper was all business in the stillness of this night in March. The dog's ears stood up straight and every so often shifted directions like a radar antenna. His nose sifted the multitude of smells of the fish market, trying to sniff out any trace of smell that did not belong. Trooper had been here before. After a while he relaxed. Everything seemed to be in order.

The officer took his large, heavy-duty flashlight from the patrol car and walked across the parking lot. He started on his routine checks, making sure that the doors of stores were properly locked, and looking for any telltale signs of forceful entry. This was mainly a business district, but there were isolated apartments in the upper stories of some of the houses.

As it was his habit, the officer let his dog run freely, knowing that Trooper would stay very close to him. There would never be a major obstacle between dog and master. Trooper did not like it and would only remain in such a position if so ordered by his handler. Hearing the dog's soft paw-steps in the dark was a very assuring sound for Vernon Scoville.

The officer concluded his inspection of the stores. Everything was in order. Scoville then proceeded towards an alley, pitchdark and quiet. The only sound was from a lonely radio in one of the few apartments.

Scoville noticed that Trooper's attention had been focused on an old bone. The officer did not want his dog to be distracted by anything during the tour of duty unless told to be "at ease." There were still a few things the young German shepherd had to learn. Scoville pitched a small pebble near the dog in order to get his attention. He did not want to call him aloud. The small pebble made a big noise, more than the officer had anticipated.

"What a noisy way to check buildings," Scoville said to himself. Trooper let go of the bone immediately and stood in front of his master within a split second. Scoville could feel the animal's intelligent eyes peer at him questioningly.

"No time for fooling around," the man whispered to his dog, and proceeded to turn into the dark alleyway. There was the backdoor of a warehouse that had to be checked.

The two were about halfway through the alley when Trooper suddenly stopped. Scoville heard him sound a low, deep growl. The dog looked toward the corner of the building in front of them and crouched, his belly almost touching the ground, as was his habit when he anticipated danger.

The officer knew that somebody or something was lurking ahead of him in the dark. He unfastened the snap on his gun holster and turned on the flashlight.

The searching light beam found a man standing about fifty feet away. The officer's first reaction was that his eyes must be playing tricks on him. The man in front of him looked like a giant. "Must be the strange shadows," Scoville thought for a second. But the level-headed police officer was not deceived. The man he confronted was over six feet tall, and weighed three hundred pounds.

The big man turned and tried to run further into the alley.

"Just stay where you are, mister!" ordered Scoville, as he and Trooper went after the man. "I've a police dog here who'd stop you in no time flat!"

Trooper growled loudly, making his point. It was certainly to the dog's credit, Scoville thought, that he did not attack. Obedience controlled instinct.

The big man stopped and turned toward the officer. He looked at the man and the dog threateningly.

Scoville noticed that the man was carrying a cloth bag. There could be only one probable explanation for his presence in the alley after three in the morning—he must have been involved in an unlawful act, probably a burglary.

"Quiet, Trooper!" Scoville ordered his dog, who stopped growling reluctantly. Actually the officer was pleased with his companion's demonstration. Then he turned to question the big man.

"What's your business here?"

"I'm on on my way home," answered the big man. "No law against that, is there?"

"Put that bag on the ground," ordered Scoville. "Then step back against the building, *all* the way."

The man did not move. He looked at the officer sullenly. This deepened Scoville's suspicion.

At this moment Trooper gave a warning bark. A car was approaching. It appeared at the end of the alley and moved toward the group.

Scoville noticed the faint trace of a malicious grin on the big man's face. Trooper became increasingly agitated, as if he felt that the balance of power was shifting to his disadvantage.

The car had a sole occupant. He stepped out, letting the motor idle, and the headlights of the car painted an eerie picture of the group. The new arrival was obviously an accomplice of the big man. The officer could tell from the attitude of the two men that the pair would not follow his orders unless forced to do so. He knew he was in for a tough job, but they were still two against two—the two suspects, and the officer with his dog.

Scoville waited for a short while to see what would happen. The man walked toward the group and came to a stop about fifteen feet from them; he had to size up the situation himself and figure out how to deal with it.

After a few seconds the new man took a couple of steps forward. Scoville and his dog were now between the newcomer and the big man. The officer realized he had to take the initiative—and fast. He stepped back to obtain a better tactical position.

"Move on, mister," Scoville addressed the newcomer. The man disregarded the order and addressed the big man.

"The cop giving you trouble?"

"A guy can't take a walk no more without some cop asking dumb questions," stated the man.

"That's enough talking," interrupted Scoville. He turned to the smaller man. "You. Against the wall!"

Scoville shifted his heavy flashlight from the right hand to the left in order to draw his gun, an action he had wanted to avoid if at all possible.

At the same instant the two suspects attacked the officer. The big man tore the heavy flashlight from Scoville's hand and smashed it against his head. The smaller man pushed the officer to the ground, knocking him almost unconscious.

It took Trooper only a fraction of a second to react. Millennia of instinct, months of training, and, probably more than anything else, the animal's complete devotion to his master, were all funnelled into the dog's furious action.

He jumped first on the three-hundred pounder, recognizing him as the more dangerous opponent. The dog's teeth sank into the man's flesh. Yelling from pain, the big man's voice tore into the stillness of the night. The smaller man produced a tire wrench and hit it with all his force against the dog's back. But, if Trooper felt any of the hammer-like blows, it did not show. He continued the attack on his victim, adding bite to bite and tear to tear.

The fury of the dog's battle was so great that the big man had to let go of the officer to defend himself. Officer Scoville was freed for a brief second, but he was on the verge of blacking out. Yet Scoville, too, acted on instinct. With all the power he could muster, he drew his gun and fired.

He found his target. The big man fell to the ground, fatally wounded.

Trooper, immediately, turned to attack the second suspect. The man, who did not like the odds, tried to make it back to his car. The dog jumped him, inflicting a severe injury on the man's right arm. The tire wrench dropped.

Trooper stopped for a second. He glanced towards his master, who tried to rise from the ground. The dog was in a quandary. Should he continue the pursuit of the attacker or, what he wanted to do so much, devote his attention to his wounded master? But Scoville solved the dog's dilemma.

"Get him!" he shouted.

The suspect was about to enter his vehicle when Trooper intercepted him with a big leap. The dog threw the man to the ground, his teeth flashing near the man's face.

"I give up!" the attacker shouted meekly. "Get the dog away from me." He surrendered willingly to the half-conscious police officer rather than face Trooper's wrath.

"Don't move then," Scoville ordered the man. "Here, Trooper!"

The dog ran to his master. He tried to lick the officer's face and hands, whining pitifully all the time, and acting as if the attack had been his fault.

"It's all right, boy," Scoville consoled his dog. "Everything is all right now. All right, thanks to you."

The officer managed to get to his feet. He intended to walk to his police car to radio for help. It seemed like a tremendous distance, for his head hurt terribly and blood was running down his face. Trooper pressed his body against his master's legs; he wanted to remain close to the officer. But there was another job for the dog.

"Guard!" ordered Scoville. Trooper, reluctantly, went back to the prisoner. His master could see through the fog of his semi-consciousness that the dog was dragging his right rear leg.

As the police officer dragged himself toward the mouth of the alley, he heard a woman calling from the second story of a building. Her attention had been attracted by the shot.

"What's going on?" she wanted to know.

"Do you have a telephone?" the badly wounded Scoville managed to shout.

"Yes, there's one in the hall."

"Then call the police," Scoville continued. "Say, 'Officer needs assistance.' "

There is no police call which gets faster response.

Scoville just hoped the woman would do what she was told, for not everyone in that neighborhood was on good terms with the police. He turned back to the suspect, who stood shivering in front of the growling Trooper. The dog knew his master was in a bad way and it was obvious that he wanted to go over and console him.

"Guard!" Scoville repeated the order, and the dog did his duty. Scoville leaned against the building, just managing to stay conscious.

Minutes later—and it seemed like hours to Scoville—there was a crescendo of police sirens, and the blinking red lights of the first squad car appeared.

The newly arrived officers took a grim inventory.

There was a dead man, showing evidence of the fury of Trooper's attack, with bites on his body, legs, and hands.

Their colleague, Officer Scoville, was bleeding from his mouth, probably in severe shock.

Pinned against the wall was the second assailant, who showed the marks of the dog's punishment.

And there was Trooper, jealously devoting all his attention to his injured master, refusing to leave his side, crying steadily.

Scoville and Trooper had done their share for this night. One of the officers retrieved Scoville's car from the parking lot in order to take him to the hospital. Scoville insisted that Trooper come along with him. The dog had some difficulty jumping into the car.

At the hospital Scoville was taken to the emergency room and treated for concussion and shock. Trooper had to stay in the squad car, where he caused a problem of his own. He refused to leave the car and he would not let any of the officers in. It seemed that he wanted to wait for his master's return. Finally Scoville's wife was able to calm down the dog and get him home. The men of the Kansas City Police Department put up patiently with

Trooper's behavior, wondering what they could do for Trooper to show their gratitude.

Officer Scoville recovered after a few days in the hospital. He credited his life to his faithful canine partner.

The second assailant recovered from the injuries inflicted on him by the dog, and was sentenced to a two- to five-year term for theft and assault.

Trooper's hind legs grew worse. An X-ray examination revealed that the dog's spine had been seriously damaged by the blows received in the fight. He gradually became completely paralyzed in the hind quarters, and soon there was no alternative but to put him out of his misery.

Trooper was buried in the Canine Corps Training Grounds of Kansas City. "Wayside Waifs, Incorporated," an animal welfare organization, presented an award to the Canine Corps in tribute to the part Trooper had played that night in March.

10

The Tiny Clue

Americans visiting their capital look with pride at the impressive federal buildings from which the fate of our nation is molded. From here, also, decisions are made affecting practically all parts of the world. But few of the visitors realize that only several hundred feet from the scrubbed monuments and glittering domes lies a different part of Washington. This area is little known except to the restless humanity forced to live there and to those who control it; this is an asphalt jungle where crime for all too many is a way of life.

Juvenile delinquents and their older tutors of crime roam the dark streets in search for a good meal, or a bottle of liquor. Less than a mile from headline-making formal receptions, robbing, beating, and assaulting are a part of the Washington night, with many misdeeds remaining unreported.

"Washington is a real time bomb," stated Robert Kennedy when he was Attorney General.

The job of preventing this time bomb from exploding rests with the Metropolitan Police Department. Under the competent guidance of its Chief, John B. Layton, modern methods of crime prevention and detection have been instituted or strengthened to check crime. One of the newer tools for this task is Washington, D.C.'s Police Canine Corps.

Even though this unit was established only in 1960, it is credited with a series of impressive successes. And, as in many other cities, the number of crimes prevented just due to the mere presence of the dogs cannot be estimated.

One of the Canine Corps' feats is especially remarkable, because the crime in question may have never been solved had it not been for an alert dog named Ben.

Early in 1962 the District of Columbia was plagued with a series of armed robberies. The bandits singled out liquor stores and paid their visits in the late evening hours.

It was nine in the evening on a Saturday night. Canine Corps handler, Tom Vincent, eased his police cruiser down a main avenue. On the back seat of the car, ears high and attentive, eyes wandering from left to right, sat the German shepherd, Ben.

Vincent watched the light traffic and listened to the routine police announcements coming over his car radio.

At that moment, three men entered a liquor store in another part of the city. The proprietor, Jack Mitchell, was alone behind the counter. For the last half hour there had been little business, even though the volume had been good earlier in the evening. Mitchell did not like the looks of the three men. With twenty years' experience, he could tell immediately whether he had a cash customer or a customer interested in his cash register. Sure enough, the three men did not waste any words. One of them drew a gun and ordered Mitchell to hand over all the money in the till.

Mitchell had no choice but to give the crooks his day's receipts, amounting to several hundred dollars. The three holdup men left the store quickly and disappeared in the dimly lit street. Mitchell put a dime into the pay telephone and called the police.

Officer Tom Vincent and his dog Ben were still continuing their routine cruise. Soon command codes flashed over the police radio, ordering two units to speed to Mitchell's Liquor Store. Vincent's car was not called. But, automatically, he made two left turns so that his car headed in the direction of the holdup scene. If he was wanted it would not take him long to respond. The decision of calling in a police dog depends on the situation when the officers and detectives arrive on the scene.

This time a dog was wanted. After a few minutes Vincent's call number sounded from the speaker, and he was ordered to the holdup store. Stepping on the gas, he turned on the red light and siren. Ben, who knew that action was to come, quivered with excitement.

"All right, you old hound," Vincent told his dog, "there may be some work cut out for us."

Ben leaned forward, putting his big head on his handler's shoulder and looking straight ahead. They were ready.

Soon Vincent's cruiser joined two squad cars and an unmarked car from the Detective Division in front of the liquor store. There was already the usual crowd of curiosity-seekers drawn away from television sets by this live action holdup.

"Always have to waste the time of at least one officer to keep the people from getting into our hair," thought Vincent while he stepped out of his car. He ordered Ben to "stay put" but, automatically, left the window open.

A detective was interrogating the proprietor when Tom Vincent entered the store. Jack Mitchell was in an understandably bad temper.

"So I just gave 'em all the dough. What else? Should I let myself get shot?"

"The only thing you could do," answered the detective, noticing Vincent from the corner of his eye.

"Hi, Tom. I called for a dog. Ben with you?"

"Sure thing," said Vincent.

"Okay," the detective continued. "Mr. Mitchell here was relieved of a few hundred dollars. Three men. I've got a description. Maybe Ben can do us some good."

Vincent knew that city tracking was an uncertain proposition under the best of circumstances. How was the dog to distinguish the scents of the three bandits from those of the customers? Vincent turned to the proprietor.

"Did you have a busy evening?"

"Quite. Especially earlier. That's why I had so much cash."

"Did anybody come into the store after the holdup?" asked Vincent.

"No. I locked the door until you people came." The man was using his head, thought Vincent, and the trail of the bandits might still be warm.

"When did the holdup take place?" Vincent asked the detective.

"Exactly at nine," came the answer.

It was now twenty-one minutes after nine. Officer Tom Vincent permitted himself a slight note of optimism. Surely, the police personnel was all over the place, and he knew that they would "mess up a trail." That could not be avoided. Also, Ben knew most of the men and understood the problem.

Tom Vincent, getting a nod from the detective, went to the door of the liquor store and called his dog. Ben, like an Olympic diver, jumped through the window in a gracious curve. A few strides later he stood next to his handler, looking at him and sounding a one-beat bark. The dog's eyes flashed with excitement.

"Come on, boy," said Vincent softly, re-entering the store with Ben close to his heels. "Go, search!" he commanded in an urgent voice. He and the dog were all business.

Jack Mitchell looked at the dog dubiously. "You don't mean to say the dog can find 'em," he said to the detective. "He may be good in a show but for this job—no. I bet those guys are already highballing it through Virginia."

"We've got to try everything," said the detective. "You never know what Ben may come up with."

While the men were talking, Ben was busy. The dog traversed the store again and again, his nose practically touching the floor.

Tom Vincent watched Ben attentively, hoping for a signal or a movement which meant that the dog had found something suspicious. But the handler left him alone. He could see the animal was having a difficult time.

Suddenly Ben gave a low bark and looked at his handler. Vincent put the leash on his dog. Ben, when on a track, had the tendency to outrun his master.

The dog pulled toward the door, with Vincent right after him. Then he made a sharp left turn. Suddenly the detective interrupted.

"No, Tom. When they took off they went in the opposite direction."

Vincent scratched the back of his head.

"Where did they come from?" he asked, turning to Mitchell.

Mitchell pointed. To him all this was a waste of time.

"They *came* from the left. When they took off they turned right."

Officer Vincent looked at Ben and motioned to him to re-enter the store.

"He may have picked up an approach scent."

"Or somebody else's," interrupted the proprietor.

Vincent patted the dog, talking to him quietly.

"Come on, Ben. Try again. See what you can find." It was more the tone of his voice than the words spoken that conveyed the message to the dog. And again Ben was busy crisscrossing the store, sorting a multitude of messages picked up by his sensitive nose, again finding the most recent one.

The dog gave another signal to track, and Vincent attached the leash. As the dog emerged from the store, he turned to the right. Ben was now straining on the leash, an indication that he was following a hot track. Vincent, the detective, and another officer followed.

Ben led the men down the street; then he crossed an alley. When he reached the parallel street he turned toward the hospital.

Vincent looked at the detective with an unhappy expression.

"You know what I think?"

" 'Fraid so. We're going to end up in a parking lot."

City tracking has its share of frustrations, for usually criminals use private or public transportation. Ben indeed entered the hospital parking lot and made a beeline to an empty parking space. But suddenly he stopped in his tracks. Barking, he retraced his steps a few dozen feet, and then went back to the spot where the trail ended. Ben looked at Vincent as if to ask for an explanation. The officer released the dog from his leash.

"That's that," Vincent muttered to himself while the detective made a few notes in his little book. "They had their getaway car here and took off."

"At least we know that," answered the detective.

"Much good it does."

Ben, in the meantime, was not idle. He ran up and down the faint trail. Suddenly he stopped and growled, attracting the attention of his master. Vincent stepped over to the dog, who tried to pick up an object from the numerous pieces of trash cluttering the edge of the parking lot. Ben growled and barked because he had some trouble getting what he wanted. But finally he turned triumphantly to Vincent with a small piece of paper in his mouth. Vincent took the piece of paper, estimating that it was about two inches square.

"They must've dropped it," he told the detective handing it to him.

"Yes," he answered. "We may be in luck yet. Good dog, Ben."

The dog was being caressed by his master. Then, as if he knew his work was done, he bounded around the half-empty parking lot like an overgrown pup, letting off steam.

The fact that Ben had looked for and found an object belonging to the bandits was no coincidence. All police dogs of the Washington, D. C., Canine Corps—and of most other police departments—are carefully trained to search for any type of article carrying the scent of the person they are tracking. However, never before in the history of police dogs had such a small piece of evidence been found by a dog and used successfully in bringing the guilty persons to justice.

The detective soon established that this small piece of paper was a bakery receipt. After many hours of searching, the bakery was located. Its owner stated that the paper in question was, of all things, a receipt for a birthday cake. He gave the officers the name and address of a young woman who had ordered the cake but never returned for it.

The officers talked to the young woman. After some hesitation she told them that she had indeed ordered the cake, but due to the illness of her mother was unable to pick it up. She had given the receipt to her boyfriend, whom she had not seen since. The officers obtained the name and address of this man.

The subject was located; he confessed to the crime and was arrested. After further questioning he implicated his two partners. All three men were identified not only by the owner of the liquor store, but also by the owners of numerous other stores who had fallen victim to these same subjects. The men were convicted and received lengthy prison terms.

Jack Mitchell, the owner of the liquor store, retrieved some of his money, and he changed his mind about dogs. So far he has not had any more trouble in his store because he is now the owner of an eighty-pound German shepherd with a mean look, mean to persons who for reasons of their own resent the dog's presence.

11

A Dog Named Duke

Officer John Tyler glanced at his speedometer. It hovered between 80 and 90. The officer was in pursuit of a Cadillac convertible that had been stolen from the parking lot of a shopping center half an hour before.

Tyler had been parked at a busy intersection when he received the signal. He had just finished adding the information about the car to his "hot sheet" when the vehicle passed by him.

"What timing!" said the officer to his dog, Duke, who was sitting attentively in the rear of the car, alerted to action by a sixth sense that never failed to amaze his master.

Officer Tyler stepped on the gas, turned on his red lights and siren. The chase was on. He reported the "make" and pursuit of the car to "Communications" over his transmitter.

The piercing siren carved a right of way out of the stream of afternoon traffic. But—as it happens so often—it helped the fugitives as well. The Cadillac gained speed and raced through two red lights, while the vehicles on the cross streets stopped obligingly.

There were five men in the convertible, wearing identical leather jackets. Tyler assumed they might be a juvenile gang bent on a joy ride.

A crisp voice cut in on the police car's speaker, ordering three additional units into the vicinity to assist. Just then, John Tyler noticed a pair of red lights blinking from the opposite direction, still a good distance away. He was not the only one to see it. The Cadillac braked down and made a sharp right into a narrow side street.

Tyler, a little later, negotiated the same turn. He picked up his microphone. "This is car 87. Continuing pursuit of suspect who turned south into Sanford. Out."

The officer knew that one of the other units would be directed to the south end of this side street. The driver of the stolen convertible must have thought the same, for he braked the car to a screeching stop. He and the other men jumped out and disappeared into an alley.

It was only ten seconds or so later that John Tyler's car came to a stop behind the Cadillac.

"Come on, Duke, get'em!" ordered the officer and the German shepherd took off into the alley. Tyler radioed in his location, and just then another police cruiser turned into Sanford Street.

John Tyler drew his gun and continued after the fugitives on foot. He could hear Duke's fortissimo bark and knew that the dog had made contact.

The five suspects were huddled against the rear wall of a garage. In front of them, Duke was taking little steps back and forth. He snarled and growled, creating the impression of an extremely ferocious animal. None of the suspects moved. As the officer approached the group he saw that they were indeed juveniles, ranging from fourteen to fifteen years of age.

The second squad car arrived on the scene, having made its way through the alley. Two officers emerged.

"Duke's doing all right for himself," one of them stated.

"Sit!" commanded Tyler and the dog followed the order, his eyes scanning the prisoners. Whenever one of the boys made the slightest movement, the animal growled and his body tensed, ready to act.

The boys looked with unconcealed hatred at the officers and their four-footed helper.

"All right, kids, it's all over," said Officer Tyler calmly. "Turn around, hands up and against the wall." The boys obeyed resignedly. On the backs of their leather jackets was the word "Grenadier," the name of one of the more troublesome juvenile gangs in town.

The suspects were frisked systematically. There was the usual harvest of switch blades and one small 22-caliber gun, unloaded.

"You can turn around now," continued Tyler easily, while one of the other officers radioed for the wagon. "We'll take a trip downtown. And no funny business. This dog can jump faster than you can think." Duke looked at Tyler understandingly and confirmed his statement with a vicious growl.

The boys were thoroughly familiar with the routine of being caught, frisked, and sent downtown. One of the things that held this group together and others like it, was hating cops. And now there was an added hate. A cop-dog. They stared at the animal with a mixture of fear and distrust—all but one of them. Duke's confirming growl to Tyler's last statement had caused this one boy to smile. He looked at the dog curiously. After a few seconds his eyes turned back to Tyler, and unconcealed hatred was again etched in the young face. Tyler stepped back from the group to talk to the officers in the other car, but he glanced again at the boy who had shown this fleeting interest in Duke. This one prisoner, he felt, did not fit into the pattern. The boy looked again at the dog with an interest that gave way to admiration. Tyler walked over to the boy and asked his name.

"Pedro Ramirez," said the suspect with a soft Mexican accent. But he had tensed as soon as the officer spoke. He was on the alert before the enemy.

"I wanna make a statement," said another boy, who turned out to be the leader and "legal expert" of the Grenadiers.

"What is it?" asked Tyler.

"This car. We didn't steal it. Just sorta borrowed it. We would'a left it, see?"

"You'll have to convince the judge," responded Officer Tyler, who was inclined to believe the boy. "But, anyway you put it, it's grand theft-auto in my book."

"Yeah. If caught you get," added Pedro Ramirez with better logic than English.

"Caught or not, it's grand theft. You boys know that," Officer Tyler said in the general direction of Pedro. "And now, let's cut out the talk."

The group was silent for awhile. John Tyler's attention was again drawn to Pedro. The boy couldn't keep his eyes off the dog.

"Your dog?" asked Pedro, interrupting the silence.

"The dog belongs to the Police Department. I'm his handler. We're together and work together all the time, though."

"Taking a dog for a walk," cut in the gang leader. "That's what us taxpayers get for our money."

Tyler didn't answer, letting the situation speak for itself. To his satisfaction he caught Pedro's glance at the speaker. Tyler knew that at least one of the members of the gang realized the worthlessness of their leader's legal talk.

A few minutes later the wagon arrived and the five juvenile delinquents started another ride downtown. Tyler and Duke stepped into their own squad car. After several more hours of work Tyler forgot all about the five Grenadiers.

About five months later Officer Tyler stopped his car in front of a hamburger stand for a fifteen-minute break.

"Stay!" he ordered Duke, who took a position next to the car. The officer walked over to the stand and ordered a hamburger.

Just then a young, dark-haired boy came along the sidewalk. As he noticed the German shepherd he slowed down, carefully examining the dog. This was not unusual, because practically everybody who saw Duke reacted with curiosity. He was an unusually beautiful animal, very big for his breed.

The boy looked first at the dog, then at the police car. After that he turned, searching for the driver. When he noted Officer Tyler, the boy's eyes showed recognition. He stood still for awhile, as if trying to make up his mind. Then he stepped hesitantly to the counter and stopped next to the policeman.

"Remember me?" he asked, after a short hesitation.

"Can't say I do," answered Tyler in a friendly way, turning and trying to connect the face with a case. From the corner of his eyes, he saw that Duke was standing up attentively. A hardly noticeable growl emerged from the dog's throat, meaning "Be careful." But Duke was always overly protective, and Tyler did not take all his danger signals seriously.

"I'm Pedro, Pedro Ramirez . . ." continued the boy. Then he looked left and right, took another step toward the policeman, and said in a low voice so that nobody else could hear, "A few months ago you catch me, I mean the dog really did."

John Tyler tapped his memory file of dozens of juvenile arrests and the face of the boy in front of him dissolved briefly to the scene in the alley . . .

"Oh yes. You and four others. The Grenadiers. Grand theft-auto . . ."

"That's right," answered Pedro, obviously delighted that he had made an impression.

"What did you get for it?" asked the officer.

"Three months. Farm," said Pedro matter-of-factly. "Not bad. Good food every day."

"Now that you're on the loose," continued the officer with unintended bitterness, "we'll have to catch you all over again."

"Not if I can help," laughed Pedro.

John Tyler looked at his watch. He still had seven minutes to go before checking in.

"Coffee?" the man asked the boy.

This was an unexpected offer coming from an officer. For a second Pedro was caught with his guard down.

"Thank you, sir," he said formally. Then, as if correcting himself, he just said, "thank you."

Tyler had difficulty holding back a little smile. Addressing an officer as "sir" was a faux pas in the juvenile delinquents' lingo.

Pedro climbed on the stool next to the policeman, looking around carefully.

"Two coffees," ordered Tyler.

Pedro had purposely arranged himself to face the street and, specifically, the dog.

Duke seemed to relax. He was sitting down again and the growling had subsided. But the animal's eyes remained on the boy.

"His name?" inquired Pedro, motioning toward the animal between two gulps of coffee.

"Duke," answered the officer.

"Good name," agreed Pedro. "How old?"

Tyler was amused by the boy's telegraphic talk. There was no waste of vocabulary.

"Two years," he answered with similar briefness.

Pedro counted on his fingers, his lips moving silently. It's probably in Spanish, guessed Tyler.

"Like me," Pedro concluded.

"Are you fourteen?" asked the officer assuming that the boy transposed dog years into human years.

"Will soon."

Officer Tyler was surprised. There was a maturity in the boy that made him look older than his age. Gained in dirty back alleys and through association with the cheapest criminal elements of the town, it was not a good type of maturity at all.

A thought crossed John Tyler's mind.

"Say, aren't you supposed to be in school?"

Pedro emptied his cup, obviously thinking for the right kind of reply.

"Between classes . . ." he telegraphed back.

Tyler let that one pass. The truant officer could worry about it. Also, this was not the time to play the tough cop. His investment in a cup of coffee to foster public relations between the Police Department and a juvenile delinquent might go down the drain. The officer paid the check.

"Time to go back on duty," he said.

"Thanks for the coffee," said the boy.

They crossed over to the dog. Pedro looked at the animal speculatively and Duke returned the look in kind.

"Okay if I pet'm?" Pedro wanted to know.

"No," answered Tyler. "He's a one-man dog. Doesn't like strangers."

"One-man dog," mused Pedro. "Good. Must be nice to have one-man dog. I had one."

"When was that?" Tyler wanted to know. He had suspected that Duke was the only reason why Pedro had sought his company. Now his suspicion was confirmed. The boy was just interested in dogs.

"Long time back," said the teenager, with his own feeling for the passage of time. "Good dog, Duke," he continued. To the policeman's amazement the German shepherd responded with the deft execution of a half cycle of a wag. For Duke, indeed, did not like strangers.

Tyler opened the door of the car and Duke jumped in. As the officer drove off, he could see through the rear view mirror a small Mexican boy looking after them with a very serious expression. But, again, Pedro Ramirez faded out of Officer Tyler's life and mind.

John Tyler and Pedro met again two months later, under less favorable circumstances. Tyler was reporting in from his day shift when he saw a number of boys lined up in the squad room.

"How's Duke?" asked one of the juveniles.

This time Tyler did not have to think twice.

"Pedro!" The boy did not seem to be embarrassed about the situation. "Duke's fine. What did they haul you in for this time?"

"I don't know, Mr. Policeman, I just don't," answered the boy with professional ease, suddenly becoming quite impersonal.

Tyler looked over the group. It was the Grenadiers again. The officer guessed the reason for Pedro's change of attitude. Two of the other boys were eyeing him curiously, and Pedro could not be burdened with the stigma of knowing a cop.

Tyler went to one of the desks where another officer was writing up the arrest report.

Pedro Ramirez and the other boys had not shown up in school for a couple of weeks. A check with Pedro's home revealed that he had not been there either. Pedro lived with his uncle, but the man was not in the least concerned about the boy's long absence.

An hour before, the boys had been located. They were living in an unoccupied one-family house. They also had an ample food supply and, so far, there was no indication of where it had come from, as none of the boys had any money.

The juveniles had been interviewed separately by an officer and they all had the same answers: they did not harm the empty house . . . food was given to them by "kind strangers" who could not be identified . . . school was a waste of time anyhow.

Tyler made arrangements to talk to Pedro alone in one of the interrogation rooms.

"What's the matter with you, Pedro? I thought you had more sense," said the officer, motioning the boy to sit down.

"Better to have less sense than be more hungry," countered Pedro with a logic of his own.

"Don't tell me your uncle lets you starve."

"No. Always spaghetti. Plenty." Pedro's expression indicated that he had eaten all the spaghetti he ever wanted.

"Had yourselves quite a time in that house you broke in," continued the officer.

"Not break in, window open," and then Pedro grinned from ear to ear, reminiscing. "Kind strangers gave good food," he rendered a rehearsed line.

"You don't think that anyone of us believes this," stated Tyler.

Pedro shrugged his shoulders in silence, indicating he could not care less whether or not anybody believed the story. He reverted to the picture of the sullen juvenile delinquent in front of his mortal enemy—the cop. But suddenly his expression changed again.

"Duke, he's all right, hm?"

"Yes," answered Tyler, "just fine."

"He catch any other . . ." Pedro was searching for the right words, ". . . . people who take car?"

"No, not for a few months," answered the officer pointedly. "But he's earning his keep."

"How?" asked the boy with unconcealed interest.

Officer Tyler could not help noticing that he was confronted with two Pedros. Pedro number one was the sullen juvenile delinquent. Pedro number two appeared when the talk turned to Duke. A light of childlike enthusiasm and interest came on then in Pedro's eyes. It must have been a problem for the boy that Tyler and Duke were a team. It would be tough to hate one and like the other.

"Well," continued Tyler, "last week he flushed a burglar from a warehouse."

"Who was he?" interrupted the boy with professional interest.

"Can't remember the name of every dumb con we catch," reacted Tyler with purpose.

"Maybe he wasn't dumb," said Pedro, taking the side of a partner in crime.

"If he had any brains he would be able to make an honest living," countered Tyler.

This point was lost on Pedro. Being honest, to him, meant not getting picked up by the police. Pedro's thoughts went back to the dog.

"Did he ever attack somebody?" he wanted to know.

"Never," stated the policeman. "He would if someone tried to attack me."

Pedro considered this statement for a while. "I wouldn't attack cop with dog. Wouldn't be right."

Officer Tyler realized only too well that it was the interest in the dog rather than respect for the law that prompted the statement.

Then the policeman got an idea.

"How would you like to see me and Duke some day when I'm off duty?"

Pedro's face was a study in conflicts. He was only too anxious to spend some time with Duke, but the price would be enormous. He would have to be with the cop.

"Duke, I much would like to see." The boy's likes and dislikes were all out in the open.

"All right," said the officer, "you can get in touch with me right here at the station. I don't know how long they'll send you away for your latest charge, but I'll still be here when you come back."

A few days after his release Pedro stood in front of the Police Station, waiting for Officer Tyler to return from his day shift.

Tyler noticed the boy from a distance. He brought his squad car to a halt before pulling into the police garage. Duke sat attentively in the rear. Pedro, Tyler thought, looked exceedingly healthy. Life on the detention farm seemed to be good for him.

"Hi there," said the officer. "Glad to see you."

"Still mean all of us meet some day?" Pedro answered directly. He talked to the officer and looked at the dog.

"That's what I said," confirmed Tyler.

They agreed to meet on the officer's next day off, a Wednesday.

"Be sure and bring Duke," emphasized the boy, as if trying to avoid the trap of meeting the policeman without his dog. Tyler put his mind at rest.

"All right. Wednesday at three in front of the 'Lido' theater. Know where it is?"

The boy nodded. Then he left with a brief wave at Duke.

When Officer Tyler approached the meeting place Pedro was waiting. He stepped into Tyler's station wagon and they took off towards the outskirts of the city.

The officer used a good part of his off duty days to give Duke a good run. The dog knew what was in store for him and was obviously excited. Pedro turned around and looked at Duke.

"Don't touch him for the time being," said the officer.

"He won't bite me," answered the boy with confidence.

"No, he won't. But we aren't going to take any chances. Let him get used to you first."

"I'm no stranger to him," answered Pedro obviously amused.

"That's what I mean," countered the officer. "The first time he met you, you were at the wrong side of his teeth."

They arrived at an open field on the south side of the town. Tyler stopped his car and they all got out. Duke was in a holiday spirit, a different animal from the serious police dog in the squad car. He barked loudly and begged his master to throw him a ball. Naturally, Duke was a perfect retriever. Tyler let Pedro toss the ball and was surprised by the distance it covered. To the boy's disappointment, the dog returned this ball to his master.

After Duke had used up some of his excess energy, Tyler had him execute a number of exercises and obedience tests, the weekly refresher course.

"Order the dog to 'sit' after I call him," suggested Tyler. He called the dog, who had been commanded to "wait" at a bench about a hundred feet away. Duke whipped around and went running to his master.

"Sit," said Pedro. There was no reaction. "Sit!" the boy said louder. But he could have saved his breath. The dog completely disregarded the boy, but looked questioningly at his master. Officer Tyler laughed at Pedro's frustration.

"Police dogs are trained to obey just one person," Tyler explained.

"Yeah," said Pedro. "We could learn the orders and use 'm."

The significance of the "we" did not go unnoticed by the police officer. He ordered Duke to "sit" and the dog obeyed immediately. "You can scratch his back if you want to. It's a good way to make friends with him."

Pedro scratched the dog's back and the boy's show of affection was accepted by the dog with aloof tolerance.

By the time this outing was over Officer John Tyler had a pretty good idea what made Pedro tick—mainly in the wrong rhythm. Also, he had looked over the boy's record, which was quite extensive and presented a rather hopeless case.

First of all, Pedro's comprehension of right and wrong was reversed. To him, the average law-abiding citizen was a "square," and the police were all wrong. His friends, minor criminals of all types, were right, and felt that the police interfered with their natural way of making a living, mainly stealing.

The boy's background was a key to his attitude. He was the son of an Irishman and a Mexican woman. The father had disappeared when Pedro was four years old, and his mother had died several years later. The boy was taken in by his mother's brother, a known petty criminal. He was not a vicious man, but more often than not there just was not enough money around to feed an ever-hungry boy.

Since his earliest youth, Pedro had been left to shift for himself. The slum district of the town became his playground, and children of similar circumstances his teachers and playmates. Going to school was distasteful to him. Teachers represented authority and ranked almost as low as the cops. Pedro played hooky whenever he could, as it was the thing to do. His uncle, obligingly, wrote letters of explanation to the principal. The list of Pedro's fictitious ailments was impressive, especially because most of them were explained in Spanish. To Pedro this procedure of deceit was correct. Teachers were there to be cheated. His uncle who, Pedro felt, was wise to the world, indicated that by his action.

One day when Pedro was about eight years old he came across a little dog in a back alley. The two started to amuse each other and found the immediate rapport only a boy and a dog can establish. When Pedro got hungry and started walking home, the dog followed him. The two became inseparable. Despite his uncle's protest, Pedro kept the dog. It was the first creature in the boy's life that cared for him completely, a feeling that was fully reciprocated.

The two had lots in common. Both came from mixed parentage. Each had only the other. Both were unwanted —until they met. Pedro had to work hard to justify the presence of the dog. But, one day, when Pedro came home from school the dog was not there. It had run away, his uncle stated. Pedro strongly suspected that the man had taken his pet away but he could never prove it. It was the first great tragedy in the boy's life, at least the first one he was fully aware of. The bitterness it created left an imprint on the youngster.

The dog episode may have led to another milestone in the boy's life, his joining the Grenadiers. Pedro did not greatly care for the boys. But, what was there to do? The Grenadiers were his only companions. They accepted him at face value at a time when he needed company. A band of about ten boys, they all had families who had been in trouble with the law and, therefore, hated cops. The boys assumed the same attitude, and it was not long until their own activities brought them in conflict with the same authorities.

There was always a need for money. Obtaining it legally never occurred to the boys. Sometimes they even worked for their elders. A youngster can make a good lookout for burglars, a messenger for numbers racketeers, an assistant to bookies, a carrier of narcotics or a transporter of stolen goods.

Enterprising youngsters like Pedro were soon carrying out their own business and the gang was a logical plat-form for the operations.

Every once in a while social workers appeared on the scene. Their limited time per case could not make much impression on the boys. Also, these people were equated with the police and were disliked accordingly. However, they could not demand the respect of the police officers who used forceful means to control them. And force was the one thing the boys understood.

John Tyler was never quite sure why he became inter-ested in Pedro. He was a practical man with no-nonsense ideas, thoroughly despising the entire stratum of crimi-nals and disagreeing with the leniency of the courts in sentencing them. Nevertheless, he continued his meet-ings with Pedro. It was Duke who played a decisive role in their relationship, for Duke accepted the boy. And Duke made only very few friends. The dog had an unfail-ing instinct about people. His power of discrimination was continually tested in a number of line-ups composed of plain citizens and suspects.

Perhaps Pedro Ramirez was not quite as bad as his atrocious police record indicated.

The boy began to like John Tyler as well, and not just as Duke's master. This came to the surface during an unexpected talk while Duke was resting after a good run in the park.

"Something I just can't dig . . ." mused the boy.

"What's that?" asked John Tyler.

"You ain't so bad . . . why did you turn cop?" asked the boy with disarming wonderment.

"Police officer," corrected Officer Tyler, who figured the time had come to work on terminology.

Pedro looked at the man as if to say "all right, if it makes you happy . . ." "Police Officer."

Tyler explained. "I was in Korea with the army. When

I came back the Force had a few openings. I made my application, took a test and was accepted."

"Was just one of'm things," the boy tried to reason out.

"No, it wasn't," answered Tyler. "I always had my eye on the Force. It's an interesting job. Always something new happening. I just couldn't sit at a desk all day."

"Me not either," added Pedro. The boy pondered for a while, still looking for some sort of justification why a perfectly nice man like Tyler would want to become a cop. Then he continued.

"Guess you was aimin' to get some dog . . ."

"When I joined," corrected Tyler, "the city didn't have any police dogs. The Canine Corps was started less than two years ago."

"What is canine?" Pedro wanted to know. It was important to him to get this part of the conversation straight.

"Canine means things to do with dogs. That's how you can easily remember it." Tyler picked up a twig from the ground and wrote "K-9" into the sand.

Pedro repeated, "Canine, canine." It was an important word to him.

Before Pedro and Tyler parted that evening, their conversation led to the Grenadiers.

"They pull a good one," bragged the boy. "But I won't tell—naturally."

"Duke and I won't be able to continue seeing you if you keep hanging around with those hoodlums," stated the officer.

Pedro let the statement sink in. He was quiet for a long time. Then, as was his habit, he hedged.

"Figure the other cops don't want *you* to be with Grenadier. Then you blame me."

"The other *police officers* are not in the least bit concerned with what I'm doing on my days off. *I* don't like it." Then he softened the blow. "You don't have to make up your mind right this minute. But don't forget!"

"Won't," said Pedro sadly. Officer Tyler felt that Duke had won a victory by making Pedro even consider the alternative. Pedro was deep in his own thoughts.

"But money I've to get," continued the boy. "You not want me steal."

"There are many honest ways a boy like you can earn some money," suggested the officer.

This idea had never occurred to the boy, but its novelty aroused his interest. He looked up at Tyler with an "I'll try everything once" expression.

"Get a newspaper route, make deliveries for a store, or be an usher in a theater. It can be done."

Every mention of a job seemed to make Pedro's face a little longer. "But that's for squares and it don't pay nothing," he remarked with disdain.

"There's one thing about those jobs. One doesn't have to be afraid of the police," remarked Tyler.

"'Fraid, 'fraid of police? Who's 'fraid of police?" reacted Pedro. Then, abruptly, he changed the subject. He handed Tyler a package he had carried with him all afternoon. The officer had begun to wonder about it.

"A present," said Pedro.

Officer Tyler unwrapped the package. It contained a small camera, worth about seventy dollars. Tyler had the odd feeling that he had just been presented with a hot camera.

"That's very nice, Pedro, but where did you get it?"

"You could take some pictures of Duke," answered Pedro disregarding the question.

"Yes, I could. But where did you get this camera?"

"What's the matter? You don't like it?" This was more evasiveness.

"I . . . I appreciate the thought but, also, I know you couldn't buy this camera."

"So, who says I buy?" continued Pedro. "I won in craps game."

Tyler and the boy went to a drugstore to get some film and took a few pictures of Duke.

The next morning, Tyler took the camera along to the station. He checked its serial number against loss reports and found that the camera was one of the numerous articles stolen during a burglary two years earlier. Tyler returned the camera to the store and the owners were impressed by the good memory of the police.

Officer John Tyler and Pedro continued meeting about once a week. While Duke was still the boy's main interest, Pedro had to admit to Tyler, "You're nice guy even if you are cop."

Pedro had to promise not to get into any trouble with the law and to go to school regularly. He had managed to keep himself out of police trouble, but his school attendance left much to be desired. He was never short of excuses. The plain truth was that the boy just hated school. Yet miraculously he managed to graduate from class to class.

One day Pedro came up with a very surprising question.

"If a guy would want to become police officer," there was great emphasis on the last two words, "what would have to happen?"

Officer Tyler knew that this was not just a speculative question, but he did not show it.

"Well, first of all one would have to be twenty-one years old. Then the person would need a high school diploma. A few years of college help, too. Good references are necessary."

"References?" Pedro asked.

"Letters by people who count. Teachers, priests, businessmen, doctors, lawyers who know the guy."

"Peoples like my uncle," added Pedro sarcastically.

"Obviously the man must have a clean record with the police," continued Tyler.

"Oh, what de hell . . ." was Pedro's summation of Tyler's statements. "And then," he continued, "one don't even be sure if a dog one gets," Pedro's English did not improve when he got excited.

"Also you've to talk very good English . . ." added Tyler inadvertently.

Pedro realized that the man had guessed the reason for his asking about the Force. He tried to lay down a smoke screen. He did it by laughing less convincingly than loud.

"Mr. Tyler, you don't think that *I* want to be cop. Me a cop. Pedro the cop." A hilarious idea, indeed.

They let the subject drop.

From that day on Pedro had a perfect attendance record in class. He studied hard and his grades improved.

One night when Tyler checked in from duty he found an urgent message in his box. Pedro was in the General Hospital, badly injured. He had been involved in a fight.

Tyler rushed to the hospital and found Pedro in one of the wards. The boy was badly mauled but not critically hurt. Pedro refused to say what had happened.

"Where is Duke?" he wanted to know. "Why didn't you bring him with you?"

Tyler explained that dogs are not usually permitted to visit patients in hospitals. Then he had a thought.

"Tell me what happened. If you do I'll try to get the dog up here. After all he's an official member of the Police Force."

It was a difficult decision for Pedro. Then the two made a compromise. The boy said he would talk if the officer promised not to use the information in any official way.

Officer Tyler agreed and listened to the story that emerged from the boy's bandaged face.

Pedro had left the Grenadiers a few weeks ago. He had not told Tyler about it. His former co-Grenadiers had become curious about the boy's change of attitude that had culminated in leaving their gang. So they put him under surveillance.

It did not take them long to discover Pedro's association with a cop—the gravest sin in their book.

That evening they had asked him to come to the high school gym, knowing from the schedule that they would have the place to themselves. Pedro did not suspect any foul play, but as soon as he appeared the boys jumped him and beat him up. Then they started to question him.

Why did he see the cop? What secrets did he spill? Was this the reason he quit the gang?

Pedro assured them that he had never talked about their activities, but they did not believe him. The boy asked them to use their heads. Had any of them been picked up and accused of anything they had done? His former colleagues had to admit that this had not happened—so far. But, who knew what would happen in the future? They wanted to pay him in advance.

They beat him up again and left Pedro unconscious in the gym. When he came to, he managed to crawl out and reach the street. A teacher who had come back to school noticed the boy and called an ambulance, very much against Pedro's wishes.

"Now what about Duke?" said Pedro faintly. Telling his story had exhausted him.

Officer Tyler went to the doctor in charge and explained the circumstances. It took considerable persuasion, but permission was obtained to bring the animal into the ward. "Just this once," emphasized the doctor.

Pedro's eyes lit up when he saw Duke. The dog, compassionately, began to lick the boy's one hand that was not in bandages.

Pedro became the hero of the ward, for Duke made a

great impression on the other patients, mainly juveniles.

"I gotta get out-a-here," said Pedro when Tyler got ready to leave. "I've a math test comin' up."

The idea that Pedro was concerned about an exam was almost too much to believe. Duke's tail gyrated. The dog always sensed when his master was in a good mood.

Pedro missed his math test. He was released from the hospital two days later none the worse for wear except for a scar on his right cheek that would stay with him all his life.

"I have a surprise for you," John Tyler told the boy when they met a few weeks later.

"What is it?" asked Pedro eagerly.

"If I told you, it wouldn't be a surprise."

"It would be, would be right now," continued the boy in his own ready logic.

"Well, just hold your horses. We're going to the Higgins place."

Mr. Higgins, as Pedro knew, was the most famous dog trainer in the area. He was also in charge of the police dog training program. Duke was a graduate of Mr. Higgins' Academy and so, in a way, was John Tyler, who received his training there in the handling of police dogs.

Mr. Higgins, who had expected Officer Tyler, received the man warmly. Then he shook hands with Pedro, who was intrigued to meet this famous person. The fact that Mr. Higgins' work was sometimes done in connection with the police did not bother the boy any longer. He had met a number of cops during the last few weeks and found they were quite decent guys.

Duke felt right at home. He obviously liked his former teacher, who scratched his back with a knowing hand. It was said of the trainer that he never used corporal punishment in the education of his dogs. His voice, on occasion, could be more cutting than the sharpest whip.

Mr. Higgins gave Tyler the run of the place. The officer showed Pedro the grounds and the training equipment. There were special ladders, some like fire escapes, high jumps and hurdles of all sizes and shapes. Pedro saw tunnels to crawl through, ditches to hide in, and a small house with special doors and windows for dogs to jump in and out.

Tyler checked Duke out on some of the more intricate maneuvers and the dog came through with flying colors. Pedro had never seen the dog perform these difficult tasks before, and he was enthralled with Duke's talents.

At last Tyler showed Pedro the actual kennels. There were all types of dogs. German shepherds were there to be tested for possible use with the Police Force, and some of them looked rather dangerous. An assortment of dogs was boarded with Mr. Higgins, usually by families who were temporarily out-of-town. Duke's presence caused a cascade of barks from various quarters but it subsided promptly after short commands by John Tyler.

They stopped at the last kennel, which contained a German shepherd, obviously very young. The dog jumped against the fence, trying to make friends with the two humans and the other canine. The two animals greeted each other with interested sniffs.

"Know who that is?" said Officer Tyler, pointing to the dog in the kennel.

The boy was intrigued. "Should I?" he asked.

Officer Tyler opened the gate and the three walked in. Pedro knelt in front of the excited dog, trying to make its acquaintance.

"One of Duke's pups, a female."

Pedro had known that Duke was used for breeding purposes and that there had been a litter about half a year ago. The male offsprings were all sold and just this little one was left.

"So, you one of the family," said Pedro, putting the

small dog's head between his hands and looking at her. After a few seconds the animal jerked her head away to perform a little dance of joy for having visitors and somebody to talk to.

"What's her name?" Pedro wanted to know.

"Princess."

"Come here, Princessa, come to Pedro," said the boy, with an apologetic look in the direction of Duke.

Here was another little dog, waiting impatiently for somebody to give her a home. Pedro must have felt this desire when he looked into the young German shepherd's shiny eyes.

"How would you like to own Princess?" came Tyler's voice.

The officer would never forget the boy's reaction. Pedro realized that this was not just conversation. He stood up, backed into the far corner of the kennel to take in the entire picture—John Tyler, Duke, and Princess, who had no idea that important decisions were in the making but ran over to Duke to nibble on one of his ears. The big dog shook his head to free himself.

Pedro remained speechless. His eyes became big. They dominated his entire face.

"Own Princess . . . ?" he finally managed to say.

"I made certain arrangements," said the officer. "You can have the dog for the asking, provided you feel you can take good care of her."

For the first time since John Tyler had met Pedro, the boy showed real emotion. Tears of joy and exictement began overflowing in the big eyes. Pedro tried to conceal this unmanly act by running over to Princess and burying his head in the young dog's fur. Then his face turned up to Tyler.

"One day I do something for you!" The boy had learned the hard law of give-and-take in the asphalt jungle where he grew up.

"There are a couple of things you must do or the dog goes back to Mr. Higgins," added Tyler.

The boy froze. He had had too many disappointments in the past in an environment where frustration was a way of life. Naturally, there was a hitch to getting the dog.

"What?" he asked militantly.

"First of all, you'll have to continue going to school regularly."

Pedro let out a sigh of relief. "That's nothing," he stated. "What else?"

"No more trouble with the law," continued Tyler.

"I stayed clean!"

"I know," said Tyler. "And you'll have to stay that way as the master of a police dog."

Pedro's tension eased. "For a minute I was scared there'd be somethin' else."

"Nothing else," answered Tyler.

Then a thought crossed Pedro's mind. "My uncle. He'll kick up fuss. But he won't get far!"

"I've thought of that," answered Tyler. "You'll have to earn enough money to feed the dog and also pay a couple of dollars rent every month. Princess won't be too difficult to care for."

"He may sell'er," continued the world-wise boy.

"He can't sell what doesn't belong to him," said the officer. "And he won't while you're paying some rent. That's the deal you'll have to make."

Pedro's right hand formed a fist. "A deal I will make and a deal he'll keep."

"We'll have to find a way for you to pick up a few dollars every week."

"Don't you worry," answered Pedro. "I know ways . . ."

John Tyler had a hard time holding back a smile. "Legit, Pedro, *legit!*"

"There aren't none. Not for me," the boy stated with complete frankness.

"Don't forget *our* deal, Pedro," stated the officer. "You've got to stay clean as a whistle if you want to keep the dog."

And it seemed that Princess understood, too. She nestled against the boy's legs and turned up her head to lick the boy's hand. It still formed a fist.

"When can I take her?" asked Pedro.

"Now," said Officer Tyler. "Run over to my car. There's a leash and collar on the back seat. They used to belong to Duke when he was smaller."

Pedro took Princess to his home. He made a deal with his uncle, though not completely along the lines anticipated by Officer Tyler.

The boy said he would pay ten dollars a month for rent and food. He would take care of the dog. Then he looked straight at his uncle and informed him with the simplicity and certainty of a slum-bred youngster: "If anything happens to Princess while I not home—I kill ya." The man knew Pedro meant business.

Pedro got himself a job with a Chinese gardener on Saturdays and Sundays. This had a number of advantages. He could take Princess along. He worked far enough from his own part of town so that none of his former pals could see that he worked like a "square." Pedro was still status conscious.

The boy's time that was not taken up by school work was devoted to Princess. There was complete rapport between the two; the dog turned out to be highly intelligent. Under the tutorship of Mr. Higgins, Officer John Tyler, and through the example set by Duke, Princess learned quickly and effortlessly to obey the basic commands.

The dog was never a problem, neither at home nor when she accompanied the boy on the gardening jobs. Princess

won the affection of everyone she met. Pedro saw to it
that she was always well groomed, and she grew into a
beautiful animal.

Princess also inherited the courage and protective instinct of her father police dog. One day the members of
the Grenadiers decided to give Pedro another beating.
The fact that the boy was going straight bothered them
no end. There was also some jealousy about the dog, who
had become the pet of the neighborhood. Pedro's friendship with a cop was the worst source of irritation. Over-
tures were made to Pedro to rejoin the gang, but they fell
on deaf ears. So, what was there to do except teach ex-
Grenadier Pedro another lesson?

The Grenadiers worked out a careful plan. They discovered that Pedro took the dog out every night. As a rule
he strolled through an alley which at that time was
deserted, training Princess to chase a ball in the dark.
It was a perfect place for an attack.

Things seemed favorable for the Grenadiers. The lookout reported that Pedro was on his way to the alley. As
the boy started tossing the ball for his dog two groups of
three Grenadiers each entered the alley from opposite
sides. Pedro was trapped without knowing it.

Somehow Princess felt that something was wrong before Pedro suspected it. The dog was chasing after a ball
when she suddenly stopped in her tracks, gave out a
warning bark and ran back to Pedro. She growled in a
way she had never done before.

At the same time Pedro noticed three figures approaching him from one side of the alley. Being wise to gang-
fights, he turned around. Surely enough, three more
shapes appeared from that side as well. All of them were
wearing sneakers, making hardly any sound.

Pedro's first concern was Princess. He had been in
fights before and knew how to take care of himself. But
what would happen to the dog?

Princess, however, had thoughts of her own. She was

concerned for her master's safety. A dormant instinct came to life and geared her into action even though she had never been in a fight before, not even with another dog.

Princess's first target were the three boys closer to Pedro. She rushed at the group with a furious snarl. The three turned and ran, but one was not fast enough, judging from an agonizing yell.

In the meantime the three boys who had advanced from the opposite direction had reached Pedro and started to hit at him. It was a brief struggle. Pedro managed to knock one of the boys to the ground. As the two remaining boys grabbed Pedro, Princess was back from her first victory and bit one of the attackers in the thigh. He let go of Pedro. The last member of the gang was not inclined to fight Pedro and the dog all by himself. He took off, with Princess snarling at his heels. The entire fight, as it was, lasted for less than a minute.

The two dog bites were never reported to the authorities, nor was Pedro ever again annoyed by any of the young hoodlums of the neighborhood.

Pedro continued to see John Tyler, although less frequently. Every once in a while they drove to the Higgins Academy for Duke's refresher courses and Princess's further training. Pedro showed an amazing patience in the handling of his dog. He knew that Princess wanted to please him and that she would do anything he asked. The only problem was finding a way to make the dog understand. Princess learned fast. It did not take her long to learn most of Duke's police work except for attack and immobilization commands. That Princess knew what to do in a pinch was amply demonstrated during the Grenadiers' attack in the dark alley.

Pedro was not a student of psychology. He acted mainly by instinct, a frame of mind acquired in his environment. John Tyler gradually became someone he both liked and respected. It was a new experience for him and, gradually, he tried to fashion himself after the man.

It was therefore not unexpected that Pedro started to think about his future, a future that included John Tyler's presence.

"Does a kid like me have a chance to become cop—I mean a police officer?" he asked. "You know I'm good with dogs. Maybe Princess and I both can join."

"It's not easy to be accepted by the Force," countered Tyler diplomatically. "I explained it to you once."

"I remember," said Pedro. "I go to school all the time," he continued with emphasis.

"So I hear," conceded the man.

"You check?"

"I check."

There was a lengthy pause until Pedro continued. It sounded suspiciously like a well-prepared argument.

"I know what you thinking," he said. "My record. Not good. But figure this way. I know my way with crooks. I know what makes 'em tick 'cause I live among them. Also, I plenty tough. None of that, if I wouldn't have record."

Pedro was enjoying the validity of the argument which had not really seemed sound to him until he heard himself expounding it. The value of making up a police force of ex-cons seemed obvious.

"Pedro, you're still a minor. Your record is not a public document," explained John Tyler. "It's kept in a sealed envelope and used only if something drastic should happen now or later. Anyhow, it's a little too soon to worry about all that. We'll have to wait until you're twenty-one."

"I know," said Pedro, counting on his fingers. "Seven years."

"That's right," said the officer. "Seven years of going to school, seven years of keeping out of trouble. And there's another thing, Pedro, you'll have to improve on the way you talk."

"Way I talk!" shouted Pedro. The ears of both Duke and Princess formed high triangles. "With my talking nothing is wrong. Everybody understands. You do. Ever not?"

"Doesn't your teacher correct you quite often?" Officer Tyler wanted to know.

"Oh, she. She must pick on somebody." Then he continued thinking out loud. "Just think me and Princess going down our street. The dog with badge on collar and me in cop-uniform. Wouldn't that be a gasser?" Pedro laughed, daydreaming about this odd experience.

Only time will tell whether or not Pedro will make it and join the Force. The men in John Tyler's precinct are pulling for the boy. Pedro's school grades are above average. His speech is improving. The big sealed envelope at juvenile court isn't getting any fatter. Still, the cloud of Pedro's past is hovering over him.

However, one thing is certain. The miraculous transition from a cop-hating kid to a youngster who wants to become a police officer was brought about by a dog named Duke.

The Author

LEO A. HANDEL was born in Vienna, Austria, and was educated in Austria, England, France, and Germany. His first major professional position was as director of audience research for Metro-Goldwyn-Mayer in New York. This job was interrupted by a stint in the U.S. Military Intelligence Service in 1944 and 1945, but afterward he returned to MGM until 1951. He then moved to Los Angeles to enter film production and is now, as president of the Handel Film Corporation, producing, writing, and directing both documentary films and theatrical features. He has the distinction of owning the most comprehensive science-film library in the field.

Mr. Handel sold his first short story when he was sixteen years old, and since then has written hundreds of works ranging from college texts on economics (in which field the versatile Mr. Handel has a Ph.D.) to comedy screenplays for TV.